CONTENTS

Life in the UK Test
Practice
Questions

Questions and answers for the
British citizenship test

....

Bo
t res
/7 —
W

Published by Red Squirrel Publishing

Red Squirrel Publishing
Suite 235, 15 Ingestre Place, London W1F 0DU, United Kingdom

www.redsquirrelbooks.com

First edition published in 2006
Thirteenth edition – First impression

Although the authors and publisher have made every effort to ensure the accuracy and completeness of information contained in this book, we assume no responsibility for errors, inaccuracies, omissions or any inconsistency herein.
A list of known errors or corrections is published at www.redsquirrelbooks.com/errata

ISBN: 978-1-907389-84-9

Edited by Henry Dillon and Alastair Smith

Proofreading by Robert Clark

Typeset by Antony Gray

Printed and bound in the UK by Micropress

INTRODUCTION

Choosing to become a British citizen is an exciting decision, one made by thousands of people each year. However, the decision to become a British citizen or permanent resident is only the start of what can be a long and challenging journey. The application process is complex, time-consuming and expensive.

Home Office statistics show that around two in ten people failed the test last year. At £50 for every test taken this is an expensive mistake, and an unnecessary one. Feedback from our customers shows that 97% pass the test using our books and other study resources.

Tens of thousands of people take the Life in the UK Test every year, but not all of them pass. However, with the right preparation, you can be one of those who passes **first time**.

About this book

This book is designed to test your knowledge and understanding of the official study materials. This introduction offers advice on how to prepare for the test and guidance on the kinds of question you will face.

There are 20 complete practice tests, each containing 24 questions in the same format as the actual test. The questions are all based on the testable sections of the official study materials, and these are the following chapters:

- The values and principles of the UK
- What is the UK?
- A long and illustrious history
- A modern, thriving society
- The UK government, the law and your role

Take some time to read through the following sections carefully. They tell you about all the features of this book and will enable you to get as much out of it as possible.

Page references

The answer tables for each practice test include a page reference to the 2022 study materials. They refer to our books: *Life in the UK Test: Handbook 2023* (ISBN: 978-1-907389-85-6) and *Life in the UK Test: Study Guide 2023* (ISBN: 978-1-907389-83-2).

These page references tell you exactly which part of the official study materials each question is based on. You can use the page references to identify difficult topics and target your study.

How to prepare for the test

1. Study the materials

The first and most important step of your preparations is to study the complete official study materials. These are found in the Home Office handbook, *Life in the United Kingdom: A guide for new residents* and are reproduced in our titles, *Life in the UK Test: Study Guide 2023* and *Life in the UK Test: Handbook 2023*. You can find more information about these books at **www.lifeintheuk.net/books**

It is essential that you read and understand the testable chapters before taking your test. Taking practice tests alone will not prepare you for the real test.

2. Take practice tests

Once you've finished thoroughly reviewing the study materials, you should check if you are ready to take the test by completing the practice tests from this book.

When you sit your official test, you will be given 45 minutes to complete the test. So when you take a practice test, you should allow yourself the same time. The pass mark in the official test is at least 75% – or up to six incorrect answers. Again, this is what you should aim to score when you take a practice test.

If you can consistently score at least 75% and finish a test within 45 minutes, then you are ready to take your official test.

If you do not pass the practice tests satisfactorily and do not feel confident enough to sit your official test you should continue your study of the testable materials. If you do not have sufficient time left before your test to do more study, then you may be able to reschedule your test appointment. You can reschedule your test without charge up to three days before the date. If you cancel your booking with less than three days' notice, your booking fee will not be refunded.

3. Online tests

Once you've finished testing yourself using the questions in this book, you can go online and access further tests with our free subscription offer.

Visit **www.lifeintheuk.net/test** and register an account to redeem this offer.

WARNING: DO NOT MEMORISE QUESTIONS

The practice questions contained in this book are intended to help you assess your understanding of the study materials and check if you are ready to take the official test.

Do not prepare for the test by memorising the questions in this book.

All the questions are in the same format as the official test questions. But they are not identical to the questions in the official test. The Home Office regularly revises the wording of questions used in the Life in the UK Test.

It is very important that you fully read and understand the study materials before taking your test.

SEND US YOUR FEEDBACK

Our books have helped hundreds of thousands of people pass the Life in the UK Test. So we're always delighted when we hear from our readers. You can send us your comments by visiting **www.lifeintheuk.net/feedback**

CHECKLIST

There are a lot of things that you need to remember to do for the Life in the UK Test. Avoid problems and get organised by completing this checklist.

☐ Test appointment booked

Book your test through the Life in the UK Test booking website **www.lituktestbooking.co.uk/lituk-web/** or by calling the Life in the UK Test Helpline on **0800 015 4245**.

Test Date   Time

Test Centre Address

Phone

☐ Finished reading study materials

☐ Completed all practice tests in this book

☐ Completed free online practice tests at **www.lifeintheuk.net**

☐ Checked latest tips and advice at **www.lifeintheuk.net**

☐ Checked your registered details exactly match your photo ID

☐ Confirmed test centre location and travel route

QUESTIONS TO EXPECT

All questions in the Life in the UK Test are multiple-choice. There are four different formats in which a question may be asked:

1. **Choose the one correct answer to the question from four options**

EXAMPLE

What important event in the development of women's rights happened in 1928?

- **A** Women were first given the right to vote
- **B** Women were given the right to vote at the same age as men
- **C** The first divorce laws were introduced
- **D** Women were allowed to keep their own earnings and property

2. **Choose two correct answers to the question from four options. You need BOTH parts to answer the question correctly**

EXAMPLE

Which TWO of the following are famous Paralympians?

- **A** Baroness Tanni Grey-Thompson
- **B** Dame Kelly Holmes
- **C** Jayne Torvill
- **D** Ellie Simmonds

3. **Decide whether a statement is true or false**

EXAMPLE

Is the statement below TRUE or FALSE?
A newspaper's owner may try to influence government policy by running a campaign.

- **A** True
- **B** False

4. Choose the correct statement from two options

EXAMPLE

Which of these statements is correct?

A Florence Nightingale is often regarded as the founder of modern nursing.

B Florence Nightingale pioneered the use of syringes in hospitals.

Working through the answers

When you start your test, make sure you read each question carefully. Make sure you understand it.

If you are confident that you know the correct answer, make your selection and move on to the next question.

It is vital that you select an answer for every question even if you are not confident that it is correct. There is a chance that even a guess will be correct! If you do this, make sure that you note the question number on your blank paper. It is possible that a question later in the test will help you to answer a question that you have found difficult.

Things to watch out for

Some questions may be worded so that an option may be a TRUE statement but not the CORRECT answer to the question being asked.

Be careful if questions and answers use words that are absolute. These words mean that the question or answer applies in all cases (e.g. *always*, *every*) or not at all (e.g. *never*).

EXAMPLE

Which of the following statements is correct?

A There are a few members of Parliament who do not represent any of the main political parties.

B Members of Parliament always belong to a political party.

The second statement is absolute. There are no exceptions. This means the correct answer is A because, whether or not there are currently independent members of Parliament (MPs) in Parliament, there *can* be independent MPs in Parliament.

You also need to be careful of words that *moderate* a question or answer. When words such as *often, rarely, sometimes* and *usually* are used, this means that the question or answer is referring to something that is not always true.

EXAMPLE

Which of the following statements is correct?

A Magistrates usually don't get paid and do not need legal qualifications.

B Magistrates must be specially trained legal experts who have been solicitors for three years.

While magistrates may be paid in some places, they usually work for free. Also, while they can have legal qualifications it is not compulsory. B is not correct in all cases, so the right answer is A.

Dates

You may get questions on dates. The study materials state you don't need to learn the dates of births and deaths, but you do have to know the dates of significant events.

EXAMPLE

When was the last successful invasion of England?

A 1066

B 1415

C 1642

D 1940

This question relates to the Norman invasion of 1066. You do need to know the dates of major events mentioned in the study materials.

EXAMPLE

Is the statement below TRUE or FALSE?
In the UK, people play practical jokes on each other on 1 April.

A True

B False

You need to know which festivals and celebrations happen on which date. Questions may cover the patron saints of the UK, religious festivals and public holidays.

The study materials say that 'Questions are based on ALL parts of the handbook, but you will not need to remember dates of birth or death' (see *The values and principles of the UK*). You must understand, however, when key events happened, or when certain individuals lived. For example, you will not be asked a question such as 'What year was Isaac Newton born in?', though you could be asked 'Which scientist, born in 1643, discovered that white light is made up of the colours of the rainbow?'

Annual events

The other exception with dates is annual events and festivals. Where something happens on the same date each year, such as Christmas or St George's Day, you must know the specific date. For moveable festivals such as Easter or Hannukah, you need to know in which months of the year they normally fall.

PRACTICE TEST 1

1   Is the statement below TRUE or FALSE?
Northern Ireland is part of Great Britain.

    A True

    B False

2   The Grand National at Aintree is an event in which sport?

    A Motor racing

    B Sailing

    C Horse racing

    D Athletics

3   Which of the following statements is correct?

    A Many civilian volunteers helped the British Navy to rescue more than 300,000 men from the beaches around Dunkirk.

    B 300,000 men were rescued from the beaches around Dunkirk solely by British Navy ships.

4   Which TWO of the following are British values based on?

    A Traditions

    B EU law

    C Party politics

    D History

5   What practice did Sake Dean Mahomet introduce to Britain?

    A Cycling

    B Drinking coffee

    C The Indian art of head massage

    D Drinking tea

6   What happens on 11 November every year?

   A Bonfire Night

   B Remembrance Day

   C Good Friday

   D Shrove Tuesday

7   Which monarch spent much of their childhood in France and was at the centre of a power struggle on their return?

   A Mary, Queen of Scots

   B Elizabeth I

   C George I

   D George II

8   The leader of the opposition appoints which of the following?

   A An alternative cabinet

   B A shadow cabinet

   C A judiciary cabinet

   D A Whig cabinet

9   Which of the following statements is correct?

   A The Scottish National Gallery is in Edinburgh.

   B The Scottish National Gallery is in Aberdeen.

10   Which of the following statements is correct?

   A Refuges and shelters offer a safe place to stay for victims of domestic violence.

   B Citizens Advice offers a safe place to stay for victims of domestic violence.

11 Which country makes up most of the total UK population?

- **A** England
- **B** Northern Ireland
- **C** Scotland
- **D** Wales

12 In which city is the Scottish Parliament based?

- **A** Sheffield
- **B** Edinburgh
- **C** Glasgow
- **D** Cardiff

13 Who suspected Mary, Queen of Scots of wanting to take the throne and kept her prisoner for 20 years?

- **A** Elizabeth I
- **B** Henry VIII
- **C** Edward VI
- **D** Charles I

14 Who wrote the Harry Potter series of books?

- **A** E L James
- **B** R L Stevenson
- **C** J K Rowling
- **D** Graham Greene

15 Why did Parliament look to restore Charles II to the throne in 1660?

- **A** There was no clear leader after the death of Oliver Cromwell
- **B** They believed in the Divine Right of Kings
- **C** They wanted a Catholic king
- **D** He wanted to give women the vote

16 Which of the following statements is correct?

   A The small claims procedure is an informal way of helping people who have been victims of identity theft or fraud.

   B The small claims procedure is an informal way of helping people settle minor disputes without needing a lawyer.

17 A snack made from flour, dried fruits and spices, and served either hot or cold is which of the following?

   A A Scottish bun

   B An English muffin

   C An Irish pie

   D A Welsh cake

18 How often must a car over three years old have an MOT test?

   A Every six months

   B Every year

   C Every three years

   D Never

19 What were women campaigning for the right to vote known as?

   A Suffragettes

   B Votettes

   C Democrettes

   D Feminettes

20 Devolved administrations in the UK control which of the following?

   A Defence policy

   B Education

   C Foreign affairs

   D Immigration

21 **Which of these is a famous UK landmark?**

A Loch Lomond and the Trossachs National Park

B Yellowstone Park

C The Brandenburg Gate

D The Black Forest

22 **To be selected to be on a jury where must your name be recorded?**

A On the voter list

B In *The Phone Book*

C On your driving licence

D On the electoral register

23 **Which of the following is a type of plane famously used in the Battle of Britain?**

A Armada

B Blitz

C Spitfire

D Concorde

24 **What does an MOT test stand for?**

A Ministry of Truth test

B Mode of Transport test

C Music and Technology test

D Ministry of Transport test

ANSWERS: PRACTICE TEST 1

			Study material reference
1	B	False	p8
2	C	Horse racing	p77
3	A	Many civilian volunteers helped the British Navy to rescue more than 300,000 men from the beaches around Dunkirk.	p49
4	A	Traditions	p2
	D	History	
5	C	The Indian art of head massage	p37
6	B	Remembrance Day	p72
7	A	Mary, Queen of Scots	p25
8	B	A shadow cabinet	p114
9	A	The Scottish National Gallery is in Edinburgh.	p82
10	A	Refuges and shelters offer a safe place to stay for victims of domestic violence.	p136
11	A	England	p65
12	B	Edinburgh	p118
13	A	Elizabeth I	p25
14	C	J K Rowling	p86
15	A	There was no clear leader after the death of Oliver Cromwell	p29–30
16	B	The small claims procedure is an informal way of helping people settle minor disputes without needing a lawyer.	p133
17	D	A Welsh cake	p90
18	B	Every year	p139
19	A	Suffragettes	p44
20	B	Education	p115
21	A	Loch Lomond and the Trossachs National Park	p99
22	D	On the electoral register	p141
23	C	Spitfire	p49
24	D	Ministry of Transport test	p139

PRACTICE TEST 2

1 Which of the following statements is correct?

    A Arranged marriages are allowed in the UK as long as the parents agree.

    B Arranged marriages are allowed in the UK as long as the people to be married agree.

2 On his escape from the Battle of Worcester, Charles II famously hid where?

    A In a barn

    B In an oak tree

    C In a cellar

    D In a church

3 Is the following statement TRUE or FALSE?
Northern Ireland and Scotland have their own banknotes, which are valid in other parts of the UK.

    A True

    B False

4 The Archbishop of Canterbury can most accurately be described as what?

    A The spiritual leader of the Church of England

    B The political leader of the Church of England

    C The administrative leader of the Church of England

    D The financial leader of the Church of England

5   The phrase 'the Dunkirk spirit' refers to which key episode of the Second World War?

   A The successful evacuation of around 300,000 men from France

   B The invasion of Italy by Allied forces

   C The British attack on the Somme

   D The bravery of the Poles throughout the war

6   Is the statement below TRUE or FALSE?
British overseas territories, such as St Helena, are part of the UK.

   A True

   B False

7   During the 18th century, new ideas about politics, philosophy and science were developed. What are these developments known as?

   A The Movement

   B The Advancement

   C The Enlightenment

   D The Regression

8   Which of the following is a purpose of the National Citizen Service programme?

   A To support the police

   B To train young people for the army

   C To help secure Britain's borders

   D To give young people an opportunity to enjoy outdoor·activities

9   To apply to become a permanent resident or citizen of the UK, you will need to be able to do which TWO of the following?

   A Speak and read English

   B Speak Welsh

   C Have a good understanding of life in the UK

   D Speak more than one language

10 Which country of the UK is not represented on the Union Flag?

   A Scotland

   B Wales

   C Northern Ireland

   D England

11 Cardiff, Swansea and Newport are cities in which country of the UK?

   A England

   B Scotland

   C Wales

   D Northern Ireland

12 In 1746 Charles Edward Stuart's attempt to replace George II as king ended with defeat at the Battle of Culloden. In which part of Britain did he raise an army?

   A Northern England

   B Southern England

   C Scotland

   D Wales

13 Which famous religious building has been the coronation church since 1066 and is the final resting place for many monarchs?

   A Westminster Abbey

   B York Minster

   C St Paul's Cathedral

   D Westminster Cathedral

14 Employment law would apply to which of the following situations?

   A Unpaid debts

   B Faulty goods bought in a shop

   C Eviction from a house or flat

   D Unfair dismissal from a job

15 Which of these birds is traditionally associated with Christmas in the UK?

- **A** Swan
- **B** Swallow
- **C** Turkey
- **D** Penguin

16 By the 1760s there were substantial British colonies in which part of the world?

- **A** North America
- **B** South America
- **C** Russia
- **D** The Middle East

17 Who wrote *The Daffodils*?

- **A** William Blake
- **B** Henry Purcell
- **C** William Wordsworth
- **D** Winston Churchill

18 Pressure and lobby groups represent the interests of which TWO of the following?

- **A** Minor political parties
- **B** Foreign ambassadors
- **C** Business organisations
- **D** Campaigning organisations

19 After his death in 1965 Winston Churchill was afforded which honour?

- **A** A state funeral
- **B** A tomb in Westminster Abbey
- **C** An annual national holiday was named after him
- **D** A burial at sea

20 **Which of the following statements is correct?**

    A The public may not listen to debates in the House of Commons or the House of Lords.

    B The public may listen to debates in the House of Commons and the House of Lords.

21 **The UK was involved in which war starting in 1899?**

    A The Crimean War

    B The Hundred Years War

    C The Boer War

    D The American War of Independence

22 **Which of the following statements is correct?**

    A The Wimbledon Championships is the only 'Grand Slam' tennis event played on clay.

    B The Wimbledon Championships is the only 'Grand Slam' tennis event played on grass.

23 **Is the statement below TRUE or FALSE?**
A jump jet capable of taking off and landing vertically was developed in the UK, and was called the Harrier.

    A True

    B False

24 **What is the name of the card that is sent to registered voters to tell them where their polling station is and when the election will take place?**

    A Poll card

    B Elector card

    C Voter card

    D Registry card

ANSWERS: PRACTICE TEST 2

			Study material reference
1	B	Arranged marriages are allowed in the UK as long as the people to be married agree.	p137
2	B	In an oak tree	p29
3	A	True	p64
4	A	The spiritual leader of the Church of England	p67
5	A	The successful evacuation of around 300,000 men from France	p49
6	B	False	p8
7	C	The Enlightenment	p35
8	D	To give young people an opportunity to enjoy outdoor activities	p145
9	A	Speak and read English	p3
	C	Have a good understanding of life in the UK	
10	B	Wales	p40
11	C	Wales	p62
12	C	Scotland	p34
13	A	Westminster Abbey	p68
14	D	Unfair dismissal from a job	p127
15	C	Turkey	p69
16	A	North America	p38
17	C	William Wordsworth	p88
18	C	Business organisations	p114
	D	Campaigning organisations	
19	A	A state funeral	p50
20	B	The public may listen to debates in the House of Commons and the House of Lords.	p122
21	C	The Boer War	p45
22	B	The Wimbledon Championships is the only 'Grand Slam' tennis event played on grass.	p78
23	A	True	p56
24	A	Poll card	p121

PRACTICE TEST 3

1 **Which TWO of the following are freedoms citizens and permanent residents of the UK should respect?**

   A Freedom of speech

   B Half-day off work on Friday

   C Freedom from unfair discrimination

   D Free heating during winter

2 **Which monarch had the longest reign of the 19th century?**

   A Victoria

   B Henry VIII

   C Edward VI

   D Anne

3 **Which events triggered England becoming a republic?**

   A The Norman Conquest and Battle of Hastings

   B The Wars of the Roses

   C The English Civil War and Oliver Cromwell's death

   D The English Civil War and Charles I's execution

4 **Which sport can be traced back to 15th century Scotland?**

   A Motor racing

   B Tennis

   C Rugby union

   D Golf

5 **Which TWO of the following are shared values of the UK?**

    A To only look after yourself

    B To obey and respect the law

    C To treat others with fairness

    D To disregard the environment

6 **Which of the following statements is correct?**

    A Having a free press means that newspaper owners may not hold political views.

    B Having a free press means that newspapers are not controlled by government.

7 **Who was Prime Minister when the Northern Ireland Assembly was elected in 1999?**

    A John Major

    B Boris Johnson

    C Tony Blair

    D Margaret Thatcher

8 **Which of the following were music hall performers who later became television stars?**

    A Margate and Wise

    B Morecambe and Wise

    C Maidstone and Wise

    D Matlock and Wise

9 **Which of these people was a great British playwright?**

    A Sir Francis Drake

    B Geoffrey Chaucer

    C William Caxton

    D William Shakespeare

10 **Which of the following takes place on 14 February every year?**

　　A St Christopher's Day

　　B St George's Day

　　C Valentine's Day

　　D All Saints Day

11 **What is the Bayeux Tapestry?**

　　A A painting

　　B An embroidery

　　C A flag

　　D A treaty

12 **Is this statement TRUE or FALSE?**
In Wales the established Church is the Church of Wales.

　　A True

　　B False

13 **The Huguenots came to Britain as refugees from which country?**

　　A Brazil

　　B Turkey

　　C Germany

　　D France

14 **Henry Moore became famous in which field of the arts?**

　　A Music

　　B Theatre

　　C Sculpture

　　D Opera

15 **Which of the following is covered by criminal law?**

A Drunk and disorderly behaviour

B Disputes with your landlord

C Employment issues such as unfair dismissal

D Debt

16 **Which TWO of these careers did Winston Churchill follow before becoming a Conservative MP in 1900?**

A Teacher

B Vicar

C Journalist

D Soldier

17 **Is the following statement TRUE or FALSE?**
Volunteering and helping your community are important parts of being a good citizen.

A True

B False

18 **Which Church of England prayer book was written during the reign of Edward VI, a version of which is still in use in some churches today?**

A The Protestant Book of Prayer

B The Roman Catholic Book of Prayer

C The Book of Common Prayer

D The Common Book of Prayer

19 **Which of the following can stand for public office?**

A Civil servants

B Members of the armed forces

C People found guilty of certain criminal offences

D British citizens born outside the UK

20 Which Prime Minister oversaw the creation of the NHS?

   A Clement Attlee

   B Winston Churchill

   C Edward Heath

   D Margaret Thatcher

21 In which year did the Battle of the Boyne take place?

   A 1590

   B 1690

   C 1960

   D 1790

22 Where was the Battle of Britain fought?

   A In the air

   B At sea

   C On the borders of Scotland

   D Underground

23 Which of the following statements is correct?

   A Benjamin Britten wrote *A Young Person's Guide to the Orchestra*.

   B Benjamin Britten wrote *An Older Person's Guide to the Orchestra*.

24 In what year were women over the age of 30 given the right to vote?

   A 1900

   B 1910

   C 1918

   D 1938

ANSWERS: PRACTICE TEST 3

			Study material reference
1	A	Freedom of speech	p3
	C	Freedom from unfair discrimination	
2	A	Victoria	p41
3	D	The English Civil War and Charles I's execution	p28–29
4	D	Golf	p77
5	B	To obey and respect the law	p140
	C	To treat others with fairness	
6	B	Having a free press means that newspapers are not controlled by government.	p119
7	C	Tony Blair	p59
8	B	Morecambe and Wise	p92
9	D	William Shakespeare	p26
10	C	Valentine's Day	p72
11	B	An embroidery	p15
12	B	False	p67
13	D	France	p34
14	C	Sculpture	p83
15	A	Drunk and disorderly behaviour	p126–127
16	C	Journalist	p50
	D	Soldier	
17	A	True	p141
18	C	The Book of Common Prayer	p24
19	D	British citizens born outside the UK	p122
20	A	Clement Attlee	p53
21	B	1690	p31
22	A	In the air	p49
23	A	Benjamin Britten wrote *A Young Person's Guide to the Orchestra*.	p80
24	C	1918	p44

PRACTICE TEST 4

1 **After his campaign in Ireland and his defeat of Charles II, Oliver Cromwell was given what title?**

- **A** King
- **B** Lord Lieutenant
- **C** Lord Protector
- **D** Chieftain

2 **What is the name of Scotland's patron saint?**

- **A** St Andrew
- **B** St David
- **C** St George
- **D** St Patrick

3 **Which of the following statements is correct?**

- **A** Tony Blair was Prime Minister at the time of the Good Friday Agreement in 1998.
- **B** Gordon Brown was Prime Minister at the time of the Good Friday Agreement in 1998.

4 **Is the statement below TRUE or FALSE?**
In Northern Ireland a system called 'individual registration' operates and all those entitled to vote must complete their own registration form.

- **A** True
- **B** False

5 **At what exact time and date in 1918 did the First World War officially end?**

A 11.00 am on 11 November

B 10.00 am on 10 October

C 6.00 am on 6 June

D 8.00 am on 8 August

6 **Which of the following statements is correct?**

A Elizabeth I was a popular monarch, particularly after the English defeat of the Spanish Armada.

B Elizabeth I was an unpopular monarch because she caused religious instability.

7 **Which of these is an environmental charity?**

A Local government

B The Council of Europe

C The London Eye

D The Eden Project

8 **Whom did William the Conqueror defeat at the Battle of Hastings in 1066?**

A King Cnut

B Boudicca

C Kenneth MacAlpin

D King Harold

9 **Where does the UK Parliament sit?**

A Westminster

B Downing Street

C Stormont

D Edinburgh Castle

10 What did missionaries teach the Anglo-Saxons?

- **A** About other cultures
- **B** About Christianity
- **C** About other languages
- **D** About trade

11 On which day do Christians paint an ash cross on their forehead as a symbol of death and sorrow for sin?

- **A** Ash Wednesday
- **B** Christmas Day
- **C** Hannukah
- **D** Remembrance Day

12 William the Conqueror came from which modern country?

- **A** Norway
- **B** Canada
- **C** Germany
- **D** France

13 Holman Hunt, Millais and Rossetti were members of which important group of 19th-century artists?

- **A** Impressionists
- **B** Expressionists
- **C** Abstract
- **D** Pre-Raphaelites

14 Young people are sent a National Insurance number before which birthday?

- **A** 13th
- **B** 15th
- **C** 16th
- **D** 18th

15 What were *The Canterbury Tales*?

   A A book of Christian doctrine

   B A series of poems

   C A Royal Charter

   D A story about Canterbury Cathedral

16 Is the following statement TRUE or FALSE?
The UK is a permanent member of the UN Security Council.

   A True

   B False

17 Is the statement below TRUE or FALSE?
The Royal Society is the oldest surviving scientific society in the world.

   A True

   B False

18 Which TWO of the following are major political parties in the UK?

   A Conservative Party

   B Social Democrats

   C Labour Party

   D Progressive Party

19 What event is commemorated on 5 November every year?

   A England's World Cup victory of 1966

   B The end of the First World War

   C A plot to blow up the Houses of Parliament

   D The Queen's birthday

20 Which of the following statements is correct?

   A Drivers over the age of 70 must renew their licence every three years.

   B People over the age of 70 are not allowed to drive.

1   Which TWO of the following countries play rugby union in the Six Nations Championship?

   A Scotland

   B France

   C New Zealand

   D Argentina

2   Who defeated the English at the Battle of Bannockburn?

   A The Welsh

   B The Irish

   C The Scottish

   D The French

3   Which of the following statements is correct?

   A Remembrance Day commemorates soldiers who died in the First World War as well as those who have died in all conflicts involving the UK since then.

   B Remembrance Day only commemorates soldiers who died in the First World War.

4   What happens at a polling station or polling place?

   A The census is collected

   B People vote in elections

   C Taxes are collected

   D People take their driving test

ANSWERS: PRACTICE TEST 4

			Study material reference
1	C	Lord Protector	p29–30
2	A	St Andrew	p68
3	A	Tony Blair was Prime Minister at the time of the Good Friday Agreement in 1998.	p59
4	A	True	p121
5	A	11.00 am on 11 November	p47
6	A	Elizabeth I was a popular monarch, particularly after the English defeat of the Spanish Armada.	p25
7	D	The Eden Project	p96
8	D	King Harold	p15
9	A	Westminster	p8
10	B	About Christianity	p14
11	A	Ash Wednesday	p70
12	D	France	p15
13	D	Pre-Raphaelites	p83
14	C	16th	p138
15	B	A series of poems	p20
16	A	True	p125
17	A	True	p30
18	A	Conservative Party	p114
	C	Labour Party	
19	C	A plot to blow up the Houses of Parliament	p72
20	A	Drivers over the age of 70 must renew their licence every three years.	p139
21	A	Scotland	p77
	B	France	
22	C	The Scottish	p17
23	A	Remembrance Day commemorates soldiers who died in the First World War as well as those who have died in all conflicts involving the UK since then.	p72
24	B	People vote in elections	p121

PRACTICE TEST 5

1   Which of the following statements is correct?

   A Elections for the Senedd are held using a first past the post system.

   B Elections for the Senedd are held using a system of proportional representation.

2   Who developed the jet engine during the 1930s?

   A Bobby Moore

   B Sir Tim Berners-Lee

   C Alan Turing

   D Sir Frank Whittle

3   Is the statement below TRUE or FALSE?
   Several Church of England bishops sit in the House of Commons.

   A True

   B False

4   Which of the following statements is correct?

   A The Scottish Parliament was formed in 1999.

   B The Scottish Parliament was formed in 2009.

5   What type of charity is Friends of the Earth?

   A Medical research

   B Environmental

   C Children's

   D Educational

6   Which of the following statements is correct?

   A The United Kingdom consists of England, Ireland, Scotland and Wales.

   B The United Kingdom consists of England, Scotland, Wales and Northern Ireland.

7   What is the name of the British athlete who has won 16 Paralympic medals, including 11 gold medals?

   A Lewis Hamilton

   B Baroness Tanni Grey-Thompson

   C Dame Kelly Holmes

   D Dame Ellen MacArthur

8   During which period were Isambard Kingdom Brunel and Florence Nightingale alive?

   A Victorian

   B Tudor

   C Middle Ages

   D The 21st century

9   Which of the following statements is correct?

   A Sir Terence Conran was a 20th century fashion designer.

   B Sir Terence Conran was a 20th century interior designer.

10   What was the Blitz?

   A Britain's departure from the EU

   B A supersonic airliner

   C Night-time bombings of British cities during the Second World War

   D A nickname for the first jet engine

11 **Is the statement below TRUE or FALSE?**
A newspaper's owner may try to influence
government policy by running a campaign.

   A True

   B False

12 **How is the British Broadcasting Corporation (BBC) funded?**

   A With money raised from TV licences

   B Through sponsorship by large national and multinational companies

   C Through advertising revenue

   D Through charitable donations

13 **Anyone who wishes to stand for public**
office must be at least what age?

   A 16

   B 18

   C 21

   D 25

14 **During the Middle Ages, which TWO languages**
were used across England?

   A Anglo-Saxon

   B Welsh

   C Danish

   D Norman French

15 **Which of the statements below is correct?**

   A Citizens must be at least 18 to vote.

   B Citizens must be at least 21 to vote.

16 **Which British novelist created the fictional detective Sherlock Holmes?**

A Sir Arthur Conan Doyle

B Evelyn Waugh

C Robert Louis Stevenson

D Graham Greene

17 **Which festival takes place on 31 October?**

A Mother's Day

B Valentine's Day

C Halloween

D St. Andrew's Day

18 **Is the statement below TRUE or FALSE?**
The Houses of Lancaster and York used red and white roses as their respective symbols.

A True

B False

19 **Is the statement below TRUE or FALSE?**
The candidate who wins the most votes in a constituency is elected as an MP.

A True

B False

20 **What was the Spanish Armada?**

A A fleet of Spanish ships

B A Spanish princess

C A treaty with Spain

D The Spanish Army

21 What is Sir Ridley Scott famous for?

   A Directing films

   B Theatre production

   C Conducting orchestras

   D Singing as an operatic tenor

22 The Church of England is a Protestant church and has existed since which event?

   A The Realisation

   B The Reformation

   C The Reorganisation

   D The Renaissance

23 What are the 40 days before Easter called?

   A Lent

   B Christmas

   C Hogmanay

   D Fast

24 Who was the first man to be called Prime Minister?

   A Sir Robert Walpole

   B William Pitt the Younger

   C Sir Herbert Walpole

   D William Pitt the Elder

ANSWERS: PRACTICE TEST 5

			Study material reference
1	B	Elections for the Senedd are held using a system of proportional representation.	p116
2	D	Sir Frank Whittle	p56
3	B	False	p67
4	A	The Scottish Parliament was formed in 1999.	p118
5	B	Environmental	p145
6	B	The United Kingdom consists of England, Scotland, Wales and Northern Ireland.	p8
7	B	Baroness Tanni Grey-Thompson	p75
8	A	Victorian	p42–43
9	B	Sir Terence Conran was a 20th century interior designer.	p85
10	C	Night-time bombings of British cities during the Second World War	p49
11	A	True	p119
12	A	With money raised from TV licences	p93
13	B	18	p122
14	A	Anglo-Saxon	p19
	D	Norman French	
15	A	Citizens must be at least 18 to vote.	p120
16	A	Sir Arthur Conan Doyle	p86
17	C	Halloween	p72
18	A	True	p21
19	A	True	p112
20	A	A fleet of Spanish ships	p25
21	A	Directing films	p90
22	B	The Reformation	p67
23	A	Lent	p70
24	A	Sir Robert Walpole	p34

PRACTICE TEST 6

1 **Which king invaded Ireland in the seventeenth century in an attempt to regain the throne with an army from France?**

- **A** Henry V
- **B** James II
- **C** Kenneth MacAlpin
- **D** John

2 **St George is the patron saint of which country?**

- **A** England
- **B** Scotland
- **C** Wales
- **D** Northern Ireland

3 **In which month do most local authorities hold elections?**

- **A** January
- **B** March
- **C** May
- **D** September

4 **Which war began after Germany invaded Poland?**

- **A** First World War
- **B** English Civil War
- **C** Second World War
- **D** Boer War

5   What celebration is known as Hogmanay in Scotland?

    A Halloween

    B Christmas

    C New Year's Eve

    D Easter

6   Is the statement below TRUE or FALSE?
Admiral Nelson was in charge of the British fleet at Trafalgar.

    A True

    B False

7   Is the following statement TRUE or FALSE?
It is compulsory for 16- and 17-year-olds to participate in the National Citizen Service programme.

    A True

    B False

8   During Hitler's bombing campaign against the UK, known as the Blitz, which of these TWO areas suffered a great deal of damage?

    A Coventry

    B Inverness

    C Falmouth

    D The East End of London

9   What is the capital city of the UK?

    A Birmingham

    B Liverpool

    C London

    D Sheffield

10 Is the statement below TRUE or FALSE?
Prince Charles is the heir to the British throne.

- **A** True
- **B** False

11 Where was William Shakespeare born?

- **A** Stratford
- **B** Stratford-upon-Avon
- **C** Bradford-on-Avon
- **D** Bradford

12 What type of television programme are
Coronation Street and *EastEnders*?

- **A** Sitcom
- **B** Documentary
- **C** Reality
- **D** Soap opera

13 The first day of one notorious battle in 1916 resulted in
60,000 British casualties. What was this battle?

- **A** The Battle of the Somme
- **B** The Battle of the Bulge
- **C** The Battle of Agincourt
- **D** The Battle of the River Plate

14 Which of the following statements is correct?

- **A** There is a National Horseracing Museum in Ascot, Berkshire.
- **B** There is a National Horseracing Museum in Newmarket, Suffolk.

15 What are members of the House of Lords known as?

- **A** MPs
- **B** Peers
- **C** Monarchs
- **D** MHLs

16 MPs have a duty to serve and represent which of the following groups?

- **A** Their fellow MPs
- **B** Everyone in their constituency
- **C** Everyone in their constituency who voted for them
- **D** The House of Lords

17 English kings fought a long war with France during the Middle Ages. What was it called?

- **A** Crimean War
- **B** Fifty Year War
- **C** Hundred Years War
- **D** Boer War

18 Is the statement below TRUE or FALSE?
It is illegal to smoke in most enclosed public spaces in the UK.

- **A** True
- **B** False

19 The first people lived in Britain during which period?

- **A** The Middle Ages
- **B** The Jurassic period
- **C** The Bronze Age
- **D** The Stone Age

20 Is the statement below TRUE or FALSE?
Eid ul Adha and Eid al-Fitr are religious festivals celebrated by Muslims in the UK.

    A True

    B False

21 What information will staff at polling stations ask voters for?

    A Who they are voting for

    B How many votes they wish to cast

    C Who their relatives are

    D Their name and address

22 Which TWO of the following are British inventions?

    A Jet engine

    B Helicopter

    C Golf cart

    D Hovercraft

23 Which of the following is a famous tennis tournament played in the UK every year?

    A Wimbledon

    B The Grand National

    C The Open

    D Six Nations

24 Which of the following is the fastest person to have sailed around the world, single-handed?

    A Dame Agatha Christie

    B Dame Mary Peters

    C Dame Kelly Holmes

    D Dame Ellen MacArthur

ANSWERS: PRACTICE TEST 6

			Study material reference
1	B	James II	p31
2	A	England	p68
3	C	May	p115
4	C	Second World War	p48–49
5	C	New Year's Eve	p72
6	A	True	p39
7	B	False	p145
8	A	Coventry	p49
	D	The East End of London	
9	C	London	p63
10	A	True	p108
11	B	Stratford-upon-Avon	p26
12	D	Soap opera	p92
13	A	The Battle of the Somme	p47
14	B	There is a National Horseracing Museum in Newmarket, Suffolk.	p77
15	B	Peers	p111
16	B	Everyone in their constituency	p112
17	C	Hundred Years War	p17
18	A	True	p126
19	D	The Stone Age	p12
20	A	True	p71
21	D	Their name and address	p121
22	A	Jet engine	p56
	D	Hovercraft	
23	A	Wimbledon	p78
24	D	Dame Ellen MacArthur	p75

PRACTICE TEST 7

1   In 1913, the British government promised 'Home Rule' for Ireland. Why was this postponed?

   A Brexit

   B The outbreak of the First World War

   C The outbreak of the Second World War

   D The Great Depression

2   What UK patron saint's name is shared with the home of golf?

   A St Andrew

   B St David

   C St Columba

   D St Patrick

3   Is the following statement TRUE or FALSE?
   Using recycled materials to make new products uses less energy and means that we do not need to extract more raw materials from the earth.

   A True

   B False

4   Which king was executed by Parliament in 1649, after losing the English Civil War?

   A William III

   B Richard III

   C Henry VIII

   D Charles I

5   The Scottish Parliament can make laws in which of the following areas?

   A Health

   B All taxes

   C Social security

   D Immigration

6   What date each year is St George's Day?

   A 23 April

   B 23 May

   C 23 June

   D 23 July

7   Which of the following statements is correct?

   A By the 18th century slavery in Britain was commonplace.

   B By the 18th century the slave trade was an established overseas industry but illegal within Britain.

8   What type of education became free under the Butler Act of 1944?

   A Nursery

   B Primary

   C Secondary

   D University

9   How are local authorities funded?

   A By funding from central government only

   B By local taxes only

   C By central government funding and by local taxes

   D Local authorities are unfunded

10 **What is the capital city of Scotland?**

A Edinburgh

B Glasgow

C Dundee

D Aberdeen

11 **Which of the following statements is correct?**

A The police must always obey the law, unless Parliament grants an exemption.

B The police must always obey the law.

12 **What did the Roman army do in AD 410?**

A Invade Ireland

B Leave Britain

C Invade Scotland

D Defeat Boudicca

13 **Which of the following statements is correct?**

A Self-employed people don't have to pay National Insurance Contributions.

B Self-employed people need to pay National Insurance Contributions themselves.

14 **Which of the following statements is correct?**

A It is legal to force someone to marry because children must obey their parents.

B It is never legal to force someone into marriage.

15 The Romans remained in Britain for how many years?

- **A** 300
- **B** 400
- **C** 500
- **D** 1,000

16 Jane Seymour gave birth to the son Henry VIII wanted. What was his name?

- **A** Henry
- **B** Edmund
- **C** Edward
- **D** Richard

17 Which of the following statements is correct?

- **A** Sir Isaac Newton was a famous scientist.
- **B** Sir Isaac Newton was a famous composer.

18 Which of the following is a benefit of volunteering?

- **A** Getting more state benefits
- **B** Getting paid
- **C** Having a chance to practise your English
- **D** A courtesy car

19 Which of the following statements is correct?

- **A** Canals were built by the Victorians who wanted to take recreational boat trips.
- **B** During the Industrial Revolution, canals were built to link factories to cities and ports.

20 **During the Middle Ages in England, parliaments were called when the king needed to consult his nobles and for what other reason?**

    A To lower taxes

    B To reform the Church of England

    C To raise money

    D To call elections

21 **Which of the following statements is correct?**

    A The UK's constitution is unwritten.

    B The UK's constitution was originally a single document, now on display in the British Library.

22 **Which of the following statements is correct?**

    A A Catholic Church of Scotland with an elected leadership was established in 1560.

    B A Protestant Church of Scotland with an elected leadership was established in 1560.

23 **Which of the following is an important festival for Muslims in the UK?**

    A Hannukah

    B Vaisakhi

    C Eid al-Fitr

    D Hogmanay

24 **Which of the following statements is correct?**

    A The jet engine and radar were developed in Britain in the 1980s.

    B The jet engine and radar were developed in Britain in the 1930s.

ANSWERS: PRACTICE TEST 7

			Study material reference
1	B	The outbreak of the First World War	p47
2	A	St Andrew	p77
3	A	True	p146
4	D	Charles I	p28
5	A	Health	p118
6	A	23 April	p68
7	B	By the 18th century the slave trade was an established overseas industry but illegal within Britain.	p37
8	C	Secondary	p54
9	C	By central government funding and by local taxes	p115
10	A	Edinburgh	p63
11	B	The police must always obey the law.	p128
12	B	Leave Britain	p13
13	B	Self-employed people need to pay National Insurance Contributions themselves.	p138
14	B	It is never legal to force someone into marriage.	p137
15	B	400	p13
16	C	Edward	p23
17	A	Sir Isaac Newton was a famous scientist.	p31
18	C	Having a chance to practise your English	p144
19	B	During the Industrial Revolution, canals were built to link factories to cities and ports.	p36–37
20	C	To raise money	p18
21	A	The UK's constitution is unwritten.	p107
22	B	A Protestant Church of Scotland with an elected leadership was established in 1560.	p25
23	C	Eid al-Fitr	p71
24	B	The jet engine and radar were developed in Britain in the 1930s.	p56

PRACTICE TEST 8

1   Which of the following is located at Holyrood?

   A The Houses of Parliament

   B The Senedd

   C The Northern Ireland Assembly

   D The Scottish Parliament

2   Which British designer was famous for Art Deco ceramics?

   A Thomas Chippendale

   B Clarice Cliff

   C Thomas Gainsborough

   D Vivienne Westwood

3   Which of the following statements is correct?

   A William Caxton was the first person in England to print books using the printing press.

   B William Caxton wrote a collection of poems in English called *The Canterbury Tales*.

4   At which of the following famous UK landmarks would you find biomes?

   A The Giant's Causeway

   B The Eden Project

   C Snowdonia

   D Edinburgh Castle

5   Is the statement below TRUE or FALSE?
   The Beveridge report of 1942 provided the basis of the modern welfare state?

   A True

   B False

6   **What does 'canvassing' for a political party mean?**

   A   To cast your vote for a party

   B   To join a party

   C   To oppose the views of the party

   D   To ask for someone's support for the party

7   **Which TWO names are used for the English translation of the Bible produced during James I's reign?**

   A   New Testament

   B   King James Version

   C   Authorised Version

   D   Old Testament

8   **Which date each year is St Andrew's Day?**

   A   30 January

   B   30 February

   C   30 November

   D   30 December

9   **Is the statement below TRUE or FALSE?**
There are a total of five notes in UK currency – £5, £10, £20, £50 and £100.

   A   True

   B   False

10   **What did hereditary peers lose in 1999?**

   A   The right to own land

   B   The automatic right to sit in the House of Lords

   C   The right to elect other peers to the House of Lords

   D   The right to speak in Parliament

11 **Is the statement below TRUE or FALSE?**
Following the Emancipation Act of 1833, the Royal Navy stopped slave ships from other countries and freed the slaves.

  A True

  B False

12 **Is the statement below TRUE or FALSE?**
Members of the House of Lords are elected by a constituency.

  A True

  B False

13 **The National Eisteddfod is a major cultural festival which takes place in which country?**

  A England

  B Scotland

  C Wales

  D Northern Ireland

14 **Is the statement below TRUE or FALSE?**
The police do not need to protect and help people who are not UK citizens.

  A True

  B False

15 **Is the following statement TRUE or FALSE?**
The Elizabethan period is remembered for the richness of its poetry and drama, especially the plays and poems of William Shakespeare.

  A True

  B False

16 Which devolved government has been suspended several times?

- **A** The Senedd
- **B** The Northern Ireland Assembly
- **C** The Scottish Parliament
- **D** The UK Parliament

17 Who was Geoffrey Chaucer?

- **A** Author of *The Canterbury Tales*
- **B** Archbishop of Canterbury
- **C** Lord Protector
- **D** Leader of the House of Commons

18 Which of the following statements is correct?

- **A** Chequers is the Prime Minister's country house.
- **B** Chequers is the Prime Minister's house in London.

19 Which of the following statements is correct?

- **A** Murder, assault and theft are crimes.
- **B** Murder, assault and theft are examples of civil disputes.

20 Where is Stormont located?

- **A** Belfast
- **B** Cardiff
- **C** London
- **D** Edinburgh

21 In 1690 William III defeated James II at which battle, which is still celebrated in Northern Ireland today?

A Battle of Bosworth Field

B Battle of the Aughrim

C Battle of Sligo

D Battle of the Boyne

22 When William of Orange became king of England, Wales, Ireland and Scotland what was the name given to this event?

A Velvet Revolution

B Glorious Revolution

C French Revolution

D Green Revolution

23 When was the Battle of Britain?

A The summer of 1899

B The summer of 1918

C The summer of 1945

D The summer of 1940

24 Decorating a tree is part of which festival celebrated in the UK?

A Halloween

B Harvest

C Easter

D Christmas

ANSWERS: PRACTICE TEST 8

			Study material reference
1	D	The Scottish Parliament	p122
2	B	Clarice Cliff	p85
3	A	William Caxton was the first person in England to print books using the printing press.	p20
4	B	The Eden Project	p96
5	A	True	p53
6	D	To ask for someone's support for the party	p143
7	B	King James Version	p27
	C	Authorised Version	
8	C	30 November	p68
9	B	False	p64
10	B	The automatic right to sit in the House of Lords	p111
11	A	True	p38
12	B	False	p111
13	C	Wales	p81
14	B	False	p128
15	A	True	p26
16	B	The Northern Ireland Assembly	p119
17	A	Author of *The Canterbury Tales*	p20
18	A	Chequers is the Prime Minister's country house.	p113
19	A	Murder, assault and theft are crimes.	p127
20	A	Belfast	p122
21	D	Battle of the Boyne	p31
22	B	Glorious Revolution	p31
23	D	The summer of 1940	p49
24	D	Christmas	p69

PRACTICE TEST 9

1   Which of the following statements is correct?

   A Members of the Northern Ireland Assembly are elected with a form of proportional representation.

   B Members of the Northern Ireland Assembly are elected using 'first past the post'.

2   What type of church is the national Church in Scotland?

   A Baptist

   B Anglican

   C Presbyterian

   D Roman Catholic

3   What improvement was made to working conditions for women and children in 1847?

   A Women and children were banned from the workplace

   B The number of hours that women and children could work was limited to 10 hours per day

   C The number of hours that women and children could work was limited to 20 hours per day

   D Women and children could only work indoors

4   In 1851, the Great Exhibition opened in Hyde Park, in which building made of iron and glass?

   A The Eiffel Tower

   B The Tower of London

   C The Crystal Palace

   D The London Eye

5   **Which of the following statements is correct?**

　　A   Serfs were free and could do as they chose.

　　B   Serfs had to work for their lord and could not move away.

6   **On which date each year is St David's day celebrated?**

　　A   1 January

　　B   1 March

　　C   1 May

　　D   1 July

7   **Which TWO of the following bands or groups are British?**

　　A   The Rolling Stones

　　B   The Jackson 5

　　C   The Beatles

　　D   The Osmonds

8   **Who decides what should happen in legal disputes over contracts, property rights or employment rights?**

　　A   The media

　　B   The police

　　C   The judiciary

　　D   The peers

9   **What was depicted in the stained glass windows of many cathedrals built in the Middle Ages?**

　　A   Stories about kings and coronations

　　B   Stories about battles and victories

　　C   Stories about the Bible and saints

　　D   Stories about communities and farming

10 What are the BAFTAs the British equivalent of?

- **A** The Victoria Cross
- **B** The Man Booker Prize
- **C** The Laurence Olivier Awards
- **D** The Oscars

11 How many crosses make up the Union Flag?

- **A** Two
- **B** Three
- **C** Four
- **D** Six

12 Which of the following statements is correct?

- **A** The UK experienced high levels of employment during the Great Depression of the 1930s.
- **B** During the Great Depression of the 1930s parts of the UK experienced mass unemployment.

13 Pumpkins, lit with candles, are used to celebrate which traditional festival?

- **A** Bonfire Night
- **B** Halloween
- **C** Midsummer
- **D** Mayday

14 Which TWO of the following are shared goals of the Commonwealth?

- **A** The rule of law
- **B** Mutual dependency
- **C** Democracy
- **D** Discrimination against non-members

15 Which of the following statements is correct?

   A When the Act of Union created the Kingdom of Great Britain, Scotland kept its own legal and education systems.

   B When the Act of Union created the Kingdom of Great Britain, Scotland adopted England's legal and education systems.

16 PCSOs support police by doing which TWO of the following?

   A Independently investigating crime

   B Patrolling the streets

   C Helping the police at crime scenes

   D Trying suspected criminals in court

17 Why was Queen Mary given the nickname 'Bloody Mary'?

   A She had red hair

   B Because of her persecution of Protestants

   C She had a bad temper

   D Because she executed her husband

18 Is the statement below TRUE or FALSE?
Employees need to pay National Insurance Contributions themselves.

   A True

   B False

19 During the reign of Henry VIII, which country of the union became formally united with England?

   A Ireland

   B Wales

   C Scotland

   D Northern Ireland

20 **What is the role of a civil servant?**

    A To deliver public services

    B To work on tobacco plantations

    C To chair debates in the House of Commons

    D To tell jokes and make fun of people in court

21 **Which of these countries was part of the British Empire during Queen Victoria's reign?**

    A France

    B Switzerland

    C The USA

    D India

22 **The longest distance in mainland Britain, at 870 miles (1,400 kilometres), is between John O'Groats and where?**

    A Land's End

    B Dover

    C Bournemouth

    D Bideford

23 **Every MP represents which of the following?**

    A A constituency

    B A county

    C A city

    D Just the people who voted for them

24 **Is the statement below TRUE or FALSE?**
Income tax pays for services such as education, roads and the armed services.

    A True

    B False

ANSWERS: PRACTICE TEST 9

			Study material reference
1	A	Members of the Northern Ireland Assembly are elected with a form of proportional representation.	p118
2	C	Presbyterian	p67
3	B	The number of hours that women and children could work was limited to 10 hours per day	p41
4	C	The Crystal Palace	p42
5	B	Serfs had to work for their lord and could not move away.	p17–18
6	B	1 March	p68
7	A	The Rolling Stones	p80
	C	The Beatles	
8	C	The judiciary	p130
9	C	Stories about the Bible and saints	p20
10	D	The Oscars	p91
11	B	Three	p40
12	B	During the Great Depression of the 1930s parts of the UK experienced mass unemployment.	p48
13	B	Halloween	p72
14	A	The rule of law	p123
	C	Democracy	
15	A	When the Act of Union created the Kingdom of Great Britain, Scotland kept its own legal and education systems.	p34
16	B	Patrolling the streets	p128
	C	Helping the police at crime scenes	
17	B	Because of her persecution of Protestants	p24
18	B	False	p138
19	B	Wales	p24
20	A	To deliver public services	p115
21	D	India	p41
22	A	Land's End	p62
23	A	A constituency	p110
24	A	True	p137

PRACTICE TEST 10

1 **Is the statement below TRUE or FALSE?**
There is no established church in Northern Ireland.

   A True

   B False

2 **Which cabinet minister is responsible for crime, policing and immigration?**

   A Foreign Secretary

   B Home Secretary

   C Defence Secretary

   D Chancellor of the Exchequer

3 **Who was the first person in England to print books using a printing press?**

   A Geoffrey Chaucer

   B Sir Francis Drake

   C William Caxton

   D Richard Arkwright

4 **The game of golf is traditionally thought to have originated in which country?**

   A England

   B Spain

   C USA

   D Scotland

5   **England declared itself a republic in 1649 after what happened?**

   A   Oliver Cromwell died

   B   Richard Cromwell became Lord Protector

   C   Charles II was crowned

   D   Charles I was executed

6   **What are MPs who don't represent a political party called?**

   A   Shadow Cabinet

   B   Ministers

   C   Civil servants

   D   Independents

7   **Which of the following pieces of legislation gave every prisoner the right to a court hearing?**

   A   The Bill of Rights

   B   The Habeas Corpus Act

   C   The Statute of Rhuddlan

   D   The Butler Act

8   **What do the words 'Magna Carta' mean?**

   A   Great Charter

   B   Freedom of Speech

   C   Bill of Rights

   D   Great King

9   **Which of the following statements is correct?**

   A   In 1703 Emmeline Pankhurst helped found the Women's Social and Political Union.

   B   In 1903 Emmeline Pankhurst helped found the Women's Social and Political Union.

10 Which of the following statements is correct?

   A The Commonwealth is a group of countries which support each other and work together.

   B The Commonwealth is a group of regions which compete together at the Olympics.

11 In the 19th century the UK became a world centre for which of the following sectors or industries?

   A Financial services

   B Agriculture

   C Wine-making

   D Entertainment

12 Where will you find Big Ben?

   A Edinburgh

   B Cardiff

   C Glasgow

   D London

13 Is the statement below TRUE or FALSE?
Norman French influenced the development of the English language as we know it today.

   A True

   B False

14 Is the statement below TRUE or FALSE?
In the UK, everybody has the right to choose their religion or choose not to practise a religion.

   A True

   B False

15 What is Stormont?

- **A** The building in which the National Assembly for Wales sits
- **B** The building in which the Scottish Parliament sits
- **C** The building in which the UK Parliament sits
- **D** The building in which the Northern Ireland Assembly sits

16 Which of the following is associated with Christmas?

- **A** Santa Claus
- **B** Sending anonymous cards
- **C** Guy Fawkes
- **D** Practical jokes

17 Is the statement below TRUE or FALSE?
St Columba became the first Archbishop of Canterbury.

- **A** True
- **B** False

18 Which of the following statements is correct?

- **A** In the UK, betting and gambling were illegal until 2005.
- **B** In the UK, betting and gambling are legal.

19 Which Anglo-Saxon poem tells of its hero's battles against monsters?

- **A** *Beowulf*
- **B** *The Fight at Finnsburh*
- **C** *Waldere*
- **D** *Deor*

20 A poll card includes which TWO pieces of information?

    A The date of the election

    B Who you should vote for

    C Where the polling station or polling place is located

    D How much tax you should pay

21 Which of the following statements is correct?

    A The Axis powers in the Second World War were Germany, Italy and Japan.

    B The Axis powers in the Second World War were Germany, Russia and China.

22 In which country is the Lake District?

    A Scotland

    B Northern Ireland

    C Wales

    D England

23 May anyone look at the electoral register?

    A No, only government officials can look at the register

    B Yes, but only under supervision

24 Which of the following statements is correct?

    A A civil servant is usually politically neutral.

    B A civil servant is always politically neutral.

ANSWERS: PRACTICE TEST 10

			Study material reference
1	A	True	p67
2	B	Home Secretary	p113
3	C	William Caxton	p20
4	D	Scotland	p77
5	D	Charles I was executed	p28–29
6	D	Independents	p114
7	B	The Habeas Corpus Act	p30
8	A	Great Charter	p18
9	B	In 1903 Emmeline Pankhurst helped found the Women's Social and Political Union.	p44
10	A	The Commonwealth is a group of countries which support each other and work together.	p123
11	A	Financial services	p42
12	D	London	p95
13	A	True	p16
14	A	True	p66
15	D	The building in which the Northern Ireland Assembly sits	p118
16	A	Santa Claus	p69
17	B	False	p15
18	B	In the UK, betting and gambling are legal.	p93–94
19	A	Beowulf	p86
20	A	The date of the election	p121
	C	Where the polling station or polling place is located	
21	A	The Axis powers in the Second World War were Germany, Italy and Japan.	p49
22	D	England	p103
23	B	Yes, but only under supervision	p121
24	B	A civil servant is always politically neutral.	p115

PRACTICE TEST 11

1   Who wrote the poem *The Tyger*?

   A Jane Austen

   B William Blake

   C William Shakespeare

   D Emmeline Pankhurst

2   How often is Prime Minister's Questions held?

   A Every day

   B Every day while Parliament is sitting

   C Every week

   D Every week while Parliament is sitting

3   A famous boat race for rowers is contested on the River Thames each year between which university teams?

   A Cambridge and London

   B Edinburgh and Oxford

   C Edinburgh and London

   D Cambridge and Oxford

4   Is the statement below TRUE or FALSE?
   You must always tell a canvasser how you intend to vote.

   A True

   B False

5   **Bobby Moore was the captain of which sports team in 1966?**

   A   Welsh rugby team

   B   English football team

   C   Scottish rugby team

   D   English cricket team

6   **Who did William III fight at the Battle of the Boyne in 1690?**

   A   Charles II

   B   Elizabeth II

   C   Henry V

   D   James II

7   **Is the statement below TRUE or FALSE?**
   The Speaker is an MP.

   A   True

   B   False

8   **Which TWO things is Sake Dean Mahomet most famous for?**

   A   Opening the first curry house in Britain

   B   Resisting British colonialism in Bengal

   C   He was a general in the Bengal army

   D   Introducing shampooing (Indian head massage) to Britain

9   **Who was Sir Edwin Lutyens?**

   A   A British architect

   B   A British composer

   C   A British swimmer

   D   A British scientist

10 **Which of the following statements is correct?**

   A A verdict of 'not proven' is possible in all UK courts.

   B A verdict of 'not proven' is only possible in Scottish courts.

11 **Is the statement below TRUE or FALSE?**
   Norwich and Bristol are cities in Wales.

   A True

   B False

12 **After the 2010 General Election saw no political party win an overall majority for the first time since 1974, the Conservative Party formed a coalition government with which party?**

   A Green Party

   B Labour Party

   C Liberal Democrats

   D UKIP

13 **What are those elected to the Scottish Parliament known as?**

   A MPs

   B Lords

   C AMs

   D MSPs

14 **Where did the Vikings form their first communities in Britain?**

   A Wales and Scotland

   B Eastern England and Scotland

   C Northern Ireland and Wales

   D South-west England and Wales

15 **Official reports of parliamentary proceedings are published in which of the following?**

   A Juilliard

   B Hansard

   C The Telegraph

   D The Sunday Times

16 **Who wrote *Charlie and the Chocolate Factory* and *George's Marvellous Medicine*?**

   A Thomas Hardy

   B Kingsley Amis

   C Roald Dahl

   D Sir Arthur Conan Doyle

17 **Which of the following statements is correct?**

   A It is legal to send a girl abroad for circumcision or cutting.

   B It is illegal in the UK to send a girl abroad for circumcision or cutting.

18 **Is the statement below TRUE or FALSE?**
The Houses of Parliament were built in the 19th century when the medieval 'gothic' style of architecture was popular.

   A True

   B False

19 **Housing, debt, employment and consumer rights are covered by which law?**

   A Civil law

   B Criminal law

   C Military law

   D No laws

20 **What is another name used for the Church of England elsewhere in the world?**

- **A** Anglican Church
- **B** Mormon Church
- **C** Zen Church
- **D** Adventist Church

21 **Is the statement below TRUE or FALSE?**
Discrimination in the workplace is covered by criminal law.

- **A** True
- **B** False

22 **Who appoints MPs to the cabinet?**

- **A** The Archbishop of Canterbury
- **B** The Queen
- **C** The Prime Minister
- **D** UK residents in a General Election

23 **Which of the following statements is correct?**

- **A** The attack on Normandy by Allied forces is often called D-Day.
- **B** D-Day was an Allied operation that attacked German forces in France by advancing through Spain.

24 **The Senedd can make laws in which of the following areas?**

- **A** Immigration
- **B** Defence
- **C** Health and social services
- **D** International trade

ANSWERS: PRACTICE TEST 11

			Study material reference
1	B	William Blake	p88
2	D	Every week while Parliament is sitting	p114
3	D	Cambridge and Oxford	p78
4	B	False	p143
5	B	English football team	p74
6	D	James II	p31
7	A	True	p111
8	A	Opening the first curry house in Britain	p37
	D	Introducing shampooing (Indian head massage) to Britain	
9	A	A British architect	p84
10	B	A verdict of 'not proven' is only possible in Scottish courts.	p130
11	B	False	p62
12	C	Liberal Democrats	p60
13	D	MSPs	p118
14	B	Eastern England and Scotland	p15
15	B	Hansard	p119
16	C	Roald Dahl	p59
17	B	It is illegal in the UK to send a girl abroad for circumcision or cutting.	p137
18	A	True	p84
19	A	Civil law	p127
20	A	Anglican Church	p67
21	B	False	p127
22	C	The Prime Minister	p113
23	A	The attack on Normandy by Allied forces is often called D-Day.	p51
24	C	Health and social services	p117

PRACTICE TEST 12

1 Where is the Children's Hearings System used to deal with children and young people who have committed an offence?

- **A** Northern Ireland
- **B** Wales
- **C** England
- **D** Scotland

2 What is the name of the swimmer who won gold medals at the 2008, 2012 and 2016 Paralympic Games?

- **A** Jayne Torvill
- **B** Dame Kelly Holmes
- **C** Ellie Simmonds
- **D** Baroness Tanni Grey-Thompson

3 The Northern Ireland Assembly can make decisions in which TWO of the following areas?

- **A** Agriculture
- **B** Nuclear energy
- **C** Foreign policy
- **D** The environment

4 Is the statement below TRUE or FALSE?
The UK government has never used its power to suspend a devolved assembly.

- **A** True
- **B** False

5   During the Victorian age how did the government promote policies of free trade?

- **A** Banning exports
- **B** Banning imports
- **C** Abolishing taxes on imported goods
- **D** Building the channel tunnel

6   What did the Act of Union create?

- **A** An official body to protect the rights of workers
- **B** The joint rule of William and Mary
- **C** The balance of power between the monarchy and Parliament
- **D** The Kingdom of Great Britain

7   Which famous UK landmark is home to the Elizabeth Tower and Big Ben?

- **A** St Paul's Cathedral
- **B** Houses of Parliament
- **C** The Tower of London
- **D** Buckingham Palace

8   Police forces are headed by whom?

- **A** Ministers
- **B** Generals
- **C** Mayors
- **D** Chief Constables

9 **What name was given to the process of removing individual small farms (crofts) in Scotland to make space for large flocks of sheep and cattle?**

- **A** The Industrial Revolution
- **B** Highland Clearances
- **C** Upland Reforms
- **D** The Enlightenment

10 **Which of the following statements is correct?**

- **A** People in the UK are living longer than ever before.
- **B** The average lifespan for UK residents is steadily decreasing.

11 **Who or what were jesters?**

- **A** Silver coins of the 18th century
- **B** Combatants on horseback at medieval feasts
- **C** People who told jokes at medieval royal courts
- **D** Men who organised hunts in the Middle Ages

12 **Which of the following statements is correct?**

- **A** You will need the help of a lawyer to issue a small claim.
- **B** You do not need the help of a lawyer to issue a small claim.

13 **Which monarch established the Church of England?**

- **A** Henry VIII
- **B** Elizabeth I
- **C** Edward I
- **D** Henry VII

14 **Is the statement below TRUE or FALSE?**
The Prime Minister appoints the cabinet.

- **A** True
- **B** False

15 Is the statement below TRUE or FALSE?
The Bayeux Tapestry commemorates a military victory for William the Conqueror.

   A True

   B False

16 What is a school's PTA?

   A Parents' trust association

   B Parent–teacher association

   C Primary Transport Agency

   D Primary teaching association

17 Which of the following statements is correct?

   A The Crimean War was the first war to receive extensive media coverage through photographs and news stories.

   B The Boer War was the first war to receive extensive media coverage through photographs and news stories.

18 Is the statement below TRUE or FALSE?
It is acceptable in the UK to discriminate against someone because of their sexuality.

   A True

   B False

19 Where did the people of the Bronze Age bury their dead?

   A Wheelbarrows

   B Round barrows

   C Cathedrals

   D Hill forts

20 If a MP resigns or dies, what is the election that is held to replace them called?

- **A** Re-election
- **B** General Election
- **C** By-election
- **D** Fresh election

21 Under which monarch did English settlers begin to colonise America?

- **A** Henry VIII
- **B** Edward II
- **C** Victoria
- **D** Elizabeth I

22 In which UK city were the 2012 Paralympic Games hosted?

- **A** Edinburgh
- **B** Swansea
- **C** Dublin
- **D** London

23 On which day is it traditional to eat pancakes?

- **A** Ash Wednesday
- **B** Shrove Tuesday
- **C** Easter Monday
- **D** Good Friday

24 Is the statement below TRUE or FALSE?
Judges are responsible for interpreting the law and ensuring that trials are conducted fairly.

- **A** True
- **B** False

ANSWERS: PRACTICE TEST 12

			Study material reference
1	D	Scotland	p131
2	C	Ellie Simmonds	p75
3	A	Agriculture	p119
	D	The environment	
4	B	False	p119
5	C	Abolishing taxes on imported goods	p41
6	D	The Kingdom of Great Britain	p34
7	B	Houses of Parliament	p95
8	D	Chief Constables	p127
9	B	Highland Clearances	p35
10	A	People in the UK are living longer than ever before.	p65
11	C	People who told jokes at medieval royal courts	p92
12	B	You do not need the help of a lawyer to issue a small claim.	p133
13	A	Henry VIII	p23
14	A	True	p113
15	A	True	p15–16
16	B	Parent–teacher association	p142
17	A	The Crimean War was the first war to receive extensive media coverage through photographs and news stories.	p42
18	B	False	p136
19	B	Round barrows	p12
20	C	By-election	p112
21	D	Elizabeth I	p26
22	D	London	p74
23	B	Shrove Tuesday	p70
24	A	True	p129

PRACTICE TEST 13

1 **Is the statement below TRUE or FALSE?**
The Black Death caused the deaths of one-third of the population of England.

   A True

   B False

2 **What is the Home Secretary responsible for?**

   A Crime, policing and immigration

   B Education

   C Defence

   D The economy

3 **Mary, Queen of Scots, was imprisoned for 20 years. How did she die?**

   A She died in childbirth

   B She was executed

   C She died of old age

   D She died in battle

4 **Is the statement below TRUE or FALSE?**
During the early 1970s, Britain admitted 28,000 people of Indian origin who had been forced to leave Uganda.

   A True

   B False

5 **Who were serfs?**

   A Soldiers in the Boer War

   B Stone age farmers

   C Peasants in Norman times who worked for a lord

   D Roman priests

6 **The Brit Awards is an annual event that gives awards in which industry?**

- **A** Television
- **B** Sport
- **C** Music
- **D** Film

7 **Is the statement below TRUE or FALSE?**
The Cenotaph in Trafalgar Square is a monument to Admiral Nelson.

- **A** True
- **B** False

8 **What is Charles Dickens famous for?**

- **A** Film directing
- **B** Designing furniture
- **C** Writing novels
- **D** Painting

9 **Which TWO of the following former colonies were granted independence in 1947?**

- **A** Pakistan
- **B** Sierra Leone
- **C** Jamaica
- **D** Ceylon (now Sri Lanka)

10 **Who was the longest-serving British Prime Minister of the 20th century?**

- **A** Boris Johnson
- **B** Winston Churchill
- **C** David Cameron
- **D** Margaret Thatcher

11 **The UK belongs to which of the following?**

    A The Women's Franchise League

    B The Australasian Union

    C The Commonwealth

    D The Arab League

12 **In 1805, Britain's navy fought combined fleets from which nations to win the Battle of Trafalgar?**

    A France and Spain

    B Spain and Italy

    C France and Italy

    D France and the Netherlands

13 **As well as giving legal advice, solicitors are able to do which TWO of the following?**

    A Represent clients in court

    B Arrest suspects

    C Take action for a client

    D Change the law

14 **The right for every adult male and female to vote is usually known as what?**

    A Universal balloting

    B Universal democracy

    C Universal voting rights

    D Universal suffrage

15 **Which of the armed forces fought in the Battle of Britain?**

- **A** Royal Air Force
- **B** Royal Navy
- **C** The Army
- **D** Royal Marines

16 **What were the Crusades?**

- **A** A fleet of ships sent from Spain to attack England
- **B** The dissolution of the monasteries by Henry VIII
- **C** The civil war between the Royalists and the Parliamentarians
- **D** The fight for control of the Holy Land by European Christians

17 **Is the statement below TRUE or FALSE?**
The Proms is a season of orchestral music that takes place every summer.

- **A** True
- **B** False

18 **Which town or city is famous for its celebration of the Hindu and Sikh festival of Diwali?**

- **A** Birmingham
- **B** Slough
- **C** Leicester
- **D** Plymouth

19 **Is the following statement TRUE or FALSE?**
England has a devolved government.

- **A** True
- **B** False

20 Charles I believed in, and tried to rule in line with, what principle?

- **A** Democracy
- **B** Communism
- **C** Religious virtue
- **D** The Divine Right of Kings

21 Is the statement below TRUE or FALSE?
A responsibility of Police and Crime Commissioners is to set local policing budgets.

- **A** True
- **B** False

22 Which famous historical event took place in 1314?

- **A** The Romans successfully invaded Britain
- **B** The Wars of the Roses began
- **C** The Battle of Bannockburn
- **D** King John signed the Magna Carta

23 Which of the following statements is correct?

- **A** To get a UK driving licence you must pass a driving test of both your knowledge and practical skills.
- **B** To get a UK driving licence you must own a car and pass a driving test of both your knowledge and practical skills.

24 Is the statement below TRUE or FALSE?
In Scotland, MSPs are elected using the 'first past the post' system.

- **A** True
- **B** False

ANSWERS: PRACTICE TEST 13

			Study material reference
1	A	True	p18
2	A	Crime, policing and immigration	p113
3	B	She was executed	p25
4	A	True	p55
5	C	Peasants in Norman times who worked for a lord	p17–18
6	C	Music	p81
7	B	False	p38
8	C	Writing novels	p86
9	A	Pakistan	p52
	D	Ceylon (now Sri Lanka)	
10	D	Margaret Thatcher	p58
11	C	The Commonwealth	p124
12	A	France and Spain	p39
13	A	Represent clients in court	p134
	C	Take action for a client	
14	D	Universal suffrage	p44
15	A	Royal Air Force	p49
16	D	The fight for control of the Holy Land by European Christians	p17
17	A	True	p79
18	C	Leicester	p70
19	B	False	p107
20	D	The Divine Right of Kings	p27
21	A	True	p127
22	C	The Battle of Bannockburn	p17
23	A	To get a UK driving licence you must pass a driving test of both your knowledge and practical skills.	p139
24	B	False	p118

PRACTICE TEST 14

1 **In May 1660 which king returned from exile in the Netherlands to restore the monarchy?**

  A John

  B Charles I

  C Henry VIII

  D Charles II

2 **How often are elections held for the Senedd?**

  A Every year

  B Every two years

  C Every five years

  D Every four years

3 **Damon Hill, Jenson Button and Lewis Hamilton are champions in which sport?**

  A Motor sport

  B Horse racing

  C Tennis

  D Squash

4 **What is the role of the Speaker in the House of Commons?**

  A To lead prayers

  B To represent the government

  C To chair debates

  D To count votes

5 Which of the following statements is correct?

A Samuel Pepys wrote a famous play during the 17th century.

B Samuel Pepys wrote a famous diary during the 17th century.

6 Is the statement below TRUE or FALSE?
A Formula 1 Grand Prix race is held in the UK every year.

A True

B False

7 Which of the following Stone Age monuments is a World Heritage Site found in Wiltshire?

A Stonehenge

B Skara Brae

C The White Tower

D Sutton Hoo

8 What is it traditional to do on 1 April in the UK?

A Play musical instruments in the street

B Play jokes on each other

C Hunt for eggs

D Make pancakes

9 Is the statement below TRUE or FALSE?
The Home Office decides who become Police and Crime Commissioners (PCC).

A True

B False

10 **Who invented the World Wide Web?**

   A Bill Gates

   B Mark Zuckerberg

   C Sir Peter Mansfield

   D Sir Tim Berners-Lee

11 **What is the name of the court that deals with minor criminal cases in England, Wales and Northern Ireland?**

   A Sheriff Court

   B Royal Court

   C Crown Court

   D Magistrates' Court

12 **Where was the first tennis club in the UK formed?**

   A Wimbledon

   B Leamington Spa

   C Bournemouth

   D Brighton

13 **Which TWO of the following countries are members of the Commonwealth?**

   A USA

   B Pakistan

   C Canada

   D Brazil

14 Which of the following statements is correct?

 A During the Elizabethan period, English settlers began to colonise America.

 B During the Elizabethan period, English settlers began to colonise Australia.

15 Is the statement below TRUE or FALSE?
The Good Friday Agreement is also known as the Belfast Agreement.

 A True

 B False

16 Which of the following statements is correct?

 A Elizabeth I succeeded Bloody Mary to become Queen of England.

 B Elizabeth I succeeded Henry VIII to become Queen of England.

17 Is the statement below TRUE or FALSE?
In Crown Courts, serious offences are tried in front of a judge and jury.

 A True

 B False

18 How were Elizabeth I and Mary, Queen of Scots related?

 A They were sisters

 B They were cousins

 C Mary was Elizabeth's daughter

 D They were half-sisters

19 Is the statement below TRUE or FALSE?
The small claims procedure is an informal way for people to settle minor disputes.

 A True

 B False

20 Who was defeated by Robert the Bruce at the Battle of Bannockburn?

   A The English

   B The Normans

   C The Romans

   D The Scottish

21 Which of the following statements is correct?

   A There are only a few charities in Britain, most of them national.

   B There are thousands of charities active in Britain.

22 Which of the following is a Jewish festival celebrating the Jews' struggle for religious freedom?

   A Vaisakhi

   B Eid al-Fitr

   C Hannukah

   D Diwali

23 How can you place your name on the electoral register?

   A By contacting your MP

   B By contacting your local council electoral registration office

   C By contacting HMRC

   D By contacting your local library

24 What type of character was Charlie Chaplin famous for playing?

   A A lawyer

   B A businessman

   C A cowboy

   D A tramp

ANSWERS: PRACTICE TEST 14

			Study material reference
1	D	Charles II	p30
2	D	Every four years	p116
3	A	Motor sport	p78
4	C	To chair debates	p111
5	B	Samuel Pepys wrote a famous diary during the 17th century.	p30
6	A	True	p78
7	A	Stonehenge	p12
8	B	Play jokes on each other	p72
9	B	False	p127
10	D	Sir Tim Berners-Lee	p57
11	D	Magistrates' Court	p130
12	B	Leamington Spa	p78
13	B	Pakistan	p124
	C	Canada	
14	A	During the Elizabethan period, English settlers began to colonise America.	p26
15	A	True	p118
16	A	Elizabeth I succeeded Bloody Mary to become Queen of England.	p24
17	A	True	p130
18	B	They were cousins	p25
19	A	True	p133
20	A	The English	p17
21	B	There are thousands of charities active in Britain.	p145
22	C	Hannukah	p71
23	B	By contacting your local council electoral registration office	p120
24	D	A tramp	p90

PRACTICE TEST 15

1 **Charles I was unwilling to reach an agreement with Parliament. Following his defeat in the English Civil War, what happened to him?**

   A He was exiled

   B He was executed

   C He was exonerated

   D He was excommunicated

2 **Is the following statement TRUE or FALSE?**
Queen Victoria's reign ended in 1952, and she was succeeded by Elizabeth II.

   A True

   B False

3 **Skara Brae is a prehistoric village found off the coast of which country?**

   A England

   B Scotland

   C France

   D Wales

4 **Which of the following provide legal advice, normally for a fee?**

   A MPs

   B Doctors

   C Solicitors

   D The police

5 **Who wrote the play *Macbeth*?**

- **A** Geoffrey Chaucer
- **B** Dame Agatha Christie
- **C** William Shakespeare
- **D** William Wordsworth

6 **Is the statement below TRUE or FALSE?**
You can only complain about the police to the Chief Constable of the police force involved.

- **A** True
- **B** False

7 **When England became a republic, after Charles I lost the English Civil War, it no longer had what?**

- **A** A parliament
- **B** A national anthem
- **C** A monarch
- **D** A Prime Minister

8 **Is the statement below TRUE or FALSE?**
The first Union Flag was created in 1606.

- **A** True
- **B** False

9 **Which of the following statements is correct?**

- **A** Thomas Chippendale was an 18th century designer of furniture.
- **B** Sir Terence Conran was an 18th century designer of furniture.

10 **Sake Dean Mahomet opened which establishment in George Street, London in 1810?**

- **A** Hindoostane Coffee House
- **B** Pakistan Curry House
- **C** Mahomet Coffee House
- **D** Mahomet Shampoo Parlour

11 **Is the statement below TRUE or FALSE?**
All MPs represent one of the main political parties.

- **A** True
- **B** False

12 **Who succeeded David Cameron to become Prime Minister on 13 July 2016?**

- **A** Margaret Thatcher
- **B** Boris Johnson
- **C** Theresa May
- **D** Winston Churchill

13 **Where in London is the White Tower?**

- **A** Tower of London
- **B** Buckingham Palace
- **C** Palace of Westminster
- **D** St Paul's Cathedral

14 **Who could not get Parliament to agree to their religious and foreign policy views and tried to rule without Parliament?**

- **A** Charles I
- **B** Elizabeth I
- **C** Bloody Mary
- **D** Henry VIII

15 Which of the following statements is correct?

A In the Northern Ireland Assembly, all ministerial offices are held by the majority party.

B In the Northern Ireland Assembly, ministerial offices are shared among the main parties.

16 Which of the following statements is correct?

A The UK has a constitutional monarchy, which means that the king or queen appoints the government, as chosen in a democratic election.

B The UK has a constitutional monarchy, which means that the king or queen alone chooses the government.

17 Which of the following is paid for by National Insurance Contributions?

A State retirement pensions

B The armed forces

C Parliamentary expenses

D The Department for Work and Pensions

18 Which of the following statements is correct?

A Many of the Viking invaders stayed in Britain, in an area known as the Danelaw.

B Many of the Viking invaders stayed in Britain, in an area known as Deptford.

19 Which TWO languages are spoken in the Senedd?

A Walloon

B English

C Welsh

D Ulster Scots

20 **Is the statement below TRUE or FALSE?**
The UK is a parliamentary democracy.

   A True

   B False

21 **Which cathedral contains a famous example of a stained glass window from the Middle Ages?**

   A Liverpool

   B Guildford

   C York Minster

   D Coventry

22 **Who did John Major succeed as Prime Minister?**

   A Tony Blair

   B Clement Attlee

   C Sir Robert Walpole

   D Margaret Thatcher

23 **Which of these is associated with Halloween?**

   A Trick or treat

   B Fireworks

   C Mistletoe

   D Hot cross buns

24 **Which German act of aggression in 1939 caused Britain and France to declare war on Germany?**

   A The invasion of Spain

   B The invasion of Russia

   C The invasion of Italy

   D The invasion of Poland

ANSWERS: PRACTICE TEST 15

			Study material reference
1	B	He was executed	p28
2	B	False	p41
3	B	Scotland	p12
4	C	Solicitors	p134–135
5	C	William Shakespeare	p26
6	B	False	p128
7	C	A monarch	p29
8	A	True	p40
9	A	Thomas Chippendale was an 18th century designer of furniture.	p85
10	A	Hindoostane Coffee House	p37
11	B	False	p114
12	C	Theresa May	p60
13	A	Tower of London	p84
14	A	Charles I	p27–28
15	B	In the Northern Ireland Assembly, ministerial offices are shared among the main parties.	p118
16	A	The UK has a constitutional monarchy, which means that the king or queen appoints the government, as chosen in a democratic election.	p107
17	A	State retirement pensions	p138
18	A	Many of the Viking invaders stayed in Britain, in an area known as the Danelaw.	p15
19	B	English	p116–117
	C	Welsh	
20	A	True	p110
21	C	York Minster	p20
22	D	Margaret Thatcher	p59
23	A	Trick or treat	p72
24	D	The invasion of Poland	p49

PRACTICE TEST 16

1 **In 1918, women over the age of 30 were given the right to vote. This was partly in recognition of the contribution women made to the war effort during which war?**

   A First World War

   B Crimean War

   C Second World War

   D Cold War

2 **Is the following statement TRUE or FALSE?**
Towns, cities and rural areas are governed by civil servants appointed by the government.

   A True

   B False

3 **What is the name of the cricket Test series played between England and Australia?**

   A The Urn

   B The Oval

   C The Ashes

   D Royal Ascot

4 **Which Jubilee did Queen Elizabeth II celebrate in 2012?**

   A Silver

   B Sapphire

   C Diamond

   D Gold

5 **Is the statement below TRUE or FALSE?**
James VI of Scotland inherited the throne of England when Elizabeth I died.

  A True

  B False

6 **Which TWO of the following names may be given to the day before Lent starts?**

  A Ash Wednesday

  B Shrove Tuesday

  C Good Friday

  D Pancake Day

7 **Which other country, alongside Britain, developed Concorde, the supersonic passenger aircraft?**

  A Germany

  B France

  C Canada

  D South Africa

8 **Which TWO of the following are famous British sportsmen or women?**

  A Baroness Tanni Grey-Thompson

  B Mary Quant

  C David Weir

  D William Beveridge

9 **Is the statement below TRUE or FALSE?**
Anyone over the age of 14 can legally buy tobacco products in the UK.

  A True

  B False

10 By 1200, the English ruled an area of Ireland around Dublin known as what?

- **A** The Light
- **B** The Pict
- **C** The Pale
- **D** The Plain

11 Snowdon is the highest mountain in which country?

- **A** England
- **B** Wales
- **C** Scotland
- **D** Northern Ireland

12 How long can you use a driving licence from another country to drive in the UK?

- **A** 2 months
- **B** 6 months
- **C** 12 months
- **D** 24 months

13 Who was William Shakespeare?

- **A** A naval commander
- **B** A Scottish patriot
- **C** An English parliamentarian
- **D** A poet, actor and playwright

14 Which monarch preceded James II?

- **A** Henry VIII
- **B** Charles II
- **C** Elizabeth II
- **D** James I

15 **During the First World War the British fought against countries including Germany, the Ottoman Empire and the Austro-Hungarian Empire. What was this alliance known as?**

- **A** The Middle Powers
- **B** The Central Powers
- **C** The Germanic Powers
- **D** The Autocratic Powers

16 **Which flower is associated with England?**

- **A** Lily
- **B** Daisy
- **C** Daffodil
- **D** Rose

17 **Which of the following great thinkers or scientists is associated with the Enlightenment?**

- **A** Edwin Lutyens
- **B** Keith Campbell
- **C** Roald Dahl
- **D** James Watt

18 **What religion was Guy Fawkes, of Gunpowder Plot fame?**

- **A** Protestant
- **B** Catholic
- **C** Methodist
- **D** Jewish

19 **Which South American country invaded the Falkland Islands in 1982?**

- **A** Peru
- **B** Argentina
- **C** Chile
- **D** Bolivia

20 **Who was king of England at the time of the Norman invasion in 1066?**

- **A** Herbert
- **B** Hubert
- **C** Harold
- **D** Henry

21 **In 1485, the Wars of the Roses ended with which battle?**

- **A** The Battle of Bolton Field
- **B** The Battle of Bakewell Field
- **C** The Battle of Bognor Field
- **D** The Battle of Bosworth Field

22 **Some people, particularly in Scotland, continued to support James II after his exile. What were these supporters called?**

- **A** Luddites
- **B** Jacobites
- **C** Monarchists
- **D** Clans

23 **What event in 1851 took place at the Crystal Palace in Hyde Park and showed goods and exhibits from Britain and across the world?**

- **A** The Great Exhibition
- **B** The Great Show
- **C** The Great Event
- **D** The Great Occasion

24 **William of Orange was the Protestant ruler of which country?**

- **A** Spain
- **B** France
- **C** The Netherlands
- **D** Portugal

ANSWERS: PRACTICE TEST 16

			Study material reference
1	A	First World War	p44
2	B	False	p115
3	C	The Ashes	p76
4	C	Diamond	p108
5	A	True	p27
6	B	Shrove Tuesday	p70
	D	Pancake Day	
7	B	France	p56
8	A	Baroness Tanni Grey-Thompson	p75
	C	David Weir	
9	B	False	p126
10	C	The Pale	p17
11	B	Wales	p101
12	C	12 months	p139
13	D	A poet, actor and playwright	p26
14	B	Charles II	p31
15	B	The Central Powers	p47
16	D	Rose	p89
17	D	James Watt	p35
18	B	Catholic	p72
19	B	Argentina	p59
20	C	Harold	p15
21	D	The Battle of Bosworth Field	p21
22	B	Jacobites	p32
23	A	The Great Exhibition	p42
24	C	The Netherlands	p31

PRACTICE TEST 17

1 **Which two of the following are required by law to give balanced coverage of rival political parties?**

- **A** Newspapers
- **B** Radio
- **C** Television
- **D** The internet

2 **Is the statement below TRUE or FALSE?**
Catherine Parr was a widow when she married Henry VIII.

- **A** True
- **B** False

3 **Which of the following statements is correct?**

- **A** The physical area that an MP represents is called a district.
- **B** The physical area that an MP represents is called a constituency.

4 **Which of the following statements is correct?**

- **A** The Cenotaph is an office building in Whitehall.
- **B** The Cenotaph is a war memorial in Whitehall.

5 **Why is Dame Jessica Ennis-Hill famous?**

- **A** She is a successful comedienne
- **B** She writes poetry
- **C** She invented the cash-dispensing ATM
- **D** She is an Olympic gold medallist

6   **Is the statement below TRUE or FALSE?**
The BBC began the world's first regular television service in 1936.

   A True

   B False

7   **Which of the following is a core value of the civil service?**

   A Laziness

   B Party loyalty

   C Integrity

   D Favouritism

8   **The Wars of the Roses were fought by the supporters of which TWO families in order to decide who should be king of England?**

   A The House of Lancaster

   B The House of Windsor

   C The House of York

   D The House of Tudor

9   **Which of the following statements is correct?**

   A Members of the public are allowed to attend Youth Court hearings.

   B Members of the public are not allowed to attend Youth Court hearings.

10   **Which of the following happened in 1707?**

   A The Act of Union was agreed, creating the Kingdom of Great Britain

   B The Hundred Years War began

   C The English Civil War ended

   D The Emancipation Act abolished slavery

11 What currency is used in the UK?

    A Euro

    B Dollar

    C Pound sterling

    D Ruble

12 Who of the following was a co-discoverer of insulin?

    A John Logie Baird

    B Sir Frank Whittle

    C John MacLeod

    D Sir Robert Watson-Watt

13 Which organisation did the UK vote to leave at a referendum on 23 June 2016?

    A United Nations

    B Commonwealth

    C European Union

    D NATO

14 Is the statement below TRUE or FALSE?
In the 17th century, Oliver Cromwell violently suppressed rebellion in Ireland and established the authority of the English Parliament.

    A True

    B False

15 Is the statement below TRUE or FALSE?
Everyone pays the correct amount of income tax through PAYE.

    A True

    B False

16 A delay in introducing Home Rule to Ireland resulted in the Easter Rising, which took place in which city?

   A Belfast

   B Dublin

   C Liverpool

   D London

17 The Boers were settlers who originally came from which country?

   A The Congo

   B The United States

   C New Zealand

   D The Netherlands

18 Who or what were the 'clans'?

   A English lords

   B Welsh landowners

   C Prominent families in Scotland and Ireland

   D Prominent families in England and Wales

19 Is the statement below TRUE or FALSE?
There are no differences between the court systems of England, Northern Ireland, Scotland and Wales.

   A True

   B False

20 Which of the following statements is correct?

   A The 1950s was a period of economic recovery and increasing prosperity for working people.

   B The 1950s was a period of economic decline that saw millions lose their jobs.

21 What is the minimum legal age to buy alcohol in a pub or night club?

  A 21

  B 25

  C 18

  D 16

22 King James I of England, Wales and Ireland was also monarch of which other country?

  A Denmark

  B Scotland

  C France

  D The Netherlands

23 Which of these sectors was nationalised by the post-war Labour government?

  A Coal mining

  B The banks

  C The airlines

  D Farming

24 With which country is Bonnie Prince Charlie associated?

  A Ireland

  B Scotland

  C France

  D Wales

ANSWERS: PRACTICE TEST 17

			Study material reference
1	B	Radio	p119
	C	Television	
2	A	True	p23
3	B	The physical area that an MP represents is called a constituency.	p110
4	B	The Cenotaph is a war memorial in Whitehall.	p84
5	D	She is an Olympic gold medallist	p75
6	A	True	p48
7	C	Integrity	p115
8	A	The House of Lancaster	p21
	C	The House of York	
9	B	Members of the public are not allowed to attend Youth Court hearings.	p131
10	A	The Act of Union was agreed, creating the Kingdom of Great Britain	p34
11	C	Pound sterling	p64
12	C	John MacLeod	p56
13	C	European Union	p60
14	A	True	p29
15	B	False	p137–138
16	B	Dublin	p47–48
17	D	The Netherlands	p45
18	C	Prominent families in Scotland and Ireland	p18
19	B	False	p130
20	A	The 1950s was a period of economic recovery and increasing prosperity for working people.	p53
21	C	18	p93
22	B	Scotland	p27
23	A	Coal mining	p52
24	B	Scotland	p34

PRACTICE TEST 18

1 **In 1954, who was the first person to run a mile in under four minutes?**

    A Sir Mo Farah

    B Sir Chris Hoy

    C Sir Roger Bannister

    D Sir Francis Chichester

2 **How many wives did Henry VIII have?**

    A One

    B Four

    C Six

    D Eight

3 **The Six Nations Championship is associated with which sport?**

    A Football

    B Cricket

    C Tennis

    D Rugby union

4 **Which of the following statements is correct?**

    A The Middle Ages was a time of peace and prosperity.

    B The Middle Ages was a time of almost constant war.

5 **Is the following statement TRUE or FALSE?**
England, Scotland and Wales have individual voting registration systems.

    A True

    B False

6 **The Victorian period famously saw reformers leading moves to improve conditions for which section of society?**

- **A** The aristocracy
- **B** The poor
- **C** The middle classes
- **D** The clergy

7 **Father's Day is celebrated in which month?**

- **A** June
- **B** July
- **C** August
- **D** September

8 **Which of the following is a core value of the Commonwealth?**

- **A** Intolerance
- **B** Slavery
- **C** Inequality
- **D** Good government

9 **On St David's Day in Wales, which flower would you expect to see people wearing?**

- **A** Daffodil
- **B** Primrose
- **C** Gladioli
- **D** Aster

10 **Which event took place shortly before the Northern Ireland Parliament was abolished in 1972?**

- **A** Britain leaving the European Union
- **B** The introduction of Home Rule
- **C** The outbreak of the Second World War
- **D** The outbreak of the Troubles

11 **Gertrude Jekyll is famous for her designs in which field?**

A Fashion

B Gardening

C Silverware

D Pottery

12 **The Chancellor of the Exchequer is responsible for which area of government policy?**

A Health

B The economy

C Defence

D Immigration

13 **Mary Stuart, the queen of Scotland, was often known by which other name?**

A Mary Tudor

B Bloody Mary

C Mary, Queen of the Highlands

D Mary, Queen of Scots

14 **Cowes on the Isle of Wight is famous for which of the following sports?**

A Rowing

B Sailing

C Fishing championships

D Surfing

15 **What effect did the Magna Carta have on the monarch?**

A It gave the monarch absolute power

B It made the monarch subject to the law

C It stripped the monarch of all power

D It had no effect

16 What is the capital city of Wales?

- **A** Newport
- **B** Cardiff
- **C** Swansea
- **D** Plymouth

17 What does every person in the UK receive, by law?

- **A** Different treatment, depending on how wealthy he or she is
- **B** Different treatment, depending on his or her job
- **C** Equal treatment
- **D** Different treatment, depending on whether the person is male or female

18 Which famous leader said the following:
'We shall fight on the beaches, we shall fight on the landing grounds, we shall fight in the fields and in the streets, we shall fight in the hills; we shall never surrender.'

- **A** Admiral Nelson
- **B** Winston Churchill
- **C** Clement Attlee
- **D** Oliver Cromwell

19 26 December is usually referred to as which of the following?

- **A** Christmas Day
- **B** New Year's Eve
- **C** St George's Day
- **D** Boxing Day

20 Which of the following statements is correct?

    A Completed ballots must be handed to an election official.

    B Completed ballots must be placed in a ballot box.

21 When was the last successful foreign invasion of England?

    A AD 789

    B 1066

    C 1940

    D 1688

22 Where is the Senedd?

    A Belfast

    B Cardiff

    C Swansea

    D Glasgow

23 Who became king after James II?

    A William III

    B Elizabeth I

    C Elizabeth II

    D Henry VIII

24 About which 20th century conflict did poets Wilfred Owen and Siegfried Sassoon write?

    A Crimean War

    B English Civil War

    C First World War

    D Second World War

ANSWERS: PRACTICE TEST 18

			Study material reference
1	C	Sir Roger Bannister	p74
2	C	Six	p23
3	D	Rugby union	p77
4	B	The Middle Ages was a time of almost constant war.	p17
5	B	False	p121
6	B	The poor	p41
7	A	June	p72
8	D	Good government	p123
9	A	Daffodil	p89
10	D	The outbreak of the Troubles	p118
11	B	Gardening	p85
12	B	The economy	p113
13	D	Mary, Queen of Scots	p25
14	B	Sailing	p78
15	B	It made the monarch subject to the law	p18
16	B	Cardiff	p63
17	C	Equal treatment	p126
18	B	Winston Churchill	p50
19	D	Boxing Day	p70
20	B	Completed ballots must be placed in a ballot box.	p121
21	B	1066	p15–16
22	B	Cardiff	p116
23	A	William III	p31
24	C	First World War	p87

PRACTICE TEST 19

1   Which one of the following is a play written by William Shakespeare?

   A *Under Milk Wood*

   B *Chariots of Fire*

   C *Macbeth*

   D *The Mousetrap*

2   Who was the first Archbishop of Canterbury?

   A St Columba

   B St Augustine

   C Winston Churchill

   D Oliver Cromwell

3   During the reign of Henry VII what happened to the power of the nobles in England?

   A It was reduced

   B It increased

   C It was abolished

   D It was absolute

4   NATO is a group of North American and European countries which have agreed to do which TWO of the following?

   A Maintain peace between member countries

   B Promote traditional culture

   C To protect each other when under attack

   D To allow the free movement of people across borders

5 **What is a way in which parents can help in schools?**

- **A** They can teach classes
- **B** They can replace the head teacher
- **C** They can do the children's homework for them
- **D** They can listen to children read in the classroom

6 **On which day do people send cards anonymously to someone they admire?**

- **A** Christmas Day
- **B** New Year's Day
- **C** Valentine's Day
- **D** April Fool's Day

7 **Why were castles built in Britain and Ireland in the Middle Ages?**

- **A** They were cheap to build
- **B** They were defensive strongholds
- **C** They were status symbols for the nobility
- **D** They created work for tradesmen

8 **Which of the following is a famous British television series?**

- **A** *Touching the Void*
- **B** *Lord of the Rings*
- **C** *In Which We Serve*
- **D** *Monty Python's Flying Circus*

9 **Which of the following statements is correct?**

- **A** Oliver Cromwell became king of England after Parliament won the Civil War.
- **B** After Parliament won the Civil War, England became a republic and Oliver Cromwell was named Lord Protector.

10 Income tax is paid on which of the following forms of income?

    A Shopping vouchers

    B Money you win on the lottery

    C Pensions

    D Small gifts of money

11 Which of the following statements is correct?

    A St Augustine and St Columba were early Christian missionaries.

    B St Augustine and St Columba were leaders who fought against the Romans.

12 Which government department collects taxes?

    A PAYE

    B NHS

    C HMRC

    D HMSO

13 Which Jewish religious festival happens in November or December every year?

    A Eid al-Fitr

    B Eid ul Adha

    C Hannukah

    D Vaisakhi

14 Is the statement below TRUE or FALSE?
Winston Churchill became Britain's Prime Minister in the early years of the Second World War.

    A True

    B False

15 Which TWO of these countries fought on the side of the Allied Powers during the First World War?

- **A** Bulgaria
- **B** Italy
- **C** Germany
- **D** France

16 Which of the following statements is correct?

- **A** In Scotland, serious offences are tried in a Sheriff Court.
- **B** In Scotland, serious offences are tried in a Crown Court.

17 Which of the following is a traditional food of Northern Ireland?

- **A** Ulster pasty
- **B** Ulster pancake
- **C** Ulster fishcake
- **D** Ulster fry

18 Which of the following is the job of the police?

- **A** To prosecute someone for being in debt
- **B** To evict noisy tenants
- **C** Representing clients in court
- **D** To protect life and property

19 On what date each year do Christians celebrate the birth of Jesus Christ?

- **A** 31 December
- **B** 1 April
- **C** 25 December
- **D** 14 February

20 The House of Lords has which of the following functions?

- **A** To appoint the Prime Minister
- **B** To hold the monarchy to account
- **C** To hire senior civil servants
- **D** To hold the government to account

21 Which Scottish poet was known as The Bard?

- **A** Robert Burns
- **B** Robert the Bruce
- **C** Bonnie Prince Charlie
- **D** Robert Davidson

22 Which of the following statements is correct?

- **A** In some areas local councils are appointed by local business owners.
- **B** Local councils are always elected.

23 King Edward I of England annexed Wales to the crown of England by which statute?

- **A** The Statute of Caernarfon
- **B** The Statute of Gwynedd
- **C** The Statute of Carmarthen
- **D** The Statute of Rhuddlan

24 Which international organisation, of which the UK is a member, was set up to promote international peace and security?

- **A** FIFA
- **B** World Health Organization
- **C** The United Nations
- **D** The Eisteddfod

ANSWERS: PRACTICE TEST 19

			Study material reference
1	C	Macbeth	p26
2	B	St Augustine	p14–15
3	A	It was reduced	p22
4	A	Maintain peace between member countries	p125
	C	To protect each other when under attack	
5	D	They can listen to children read in the classroom	p141
6	C	Valentine's Day	p72
7	B	They were defensive strongholds	p20
8	D	*Monty Python's Flying Circus*	p92
9	B	After Parliament won the Civil War, England became a republic and Oliver Cromwell was named Lord Protector.	p29–30
10	C	Pensions	p137
11	A	St Augustine and St Columba were early Christian missionaries.	p14–15
12	C	HMRC	p137–138
13	C	Hannukah	p71
14	A	True	p49
15	B	Italy	p47
	D	France	
16	A	In Scotland, serious offences are tried in a Sheriff Court.	p130
17	D	Ulster fry	p90
18	D	To protect life and property	p127
19	C	25 December	p69
20	D	To hold the government to account	p111
21	A	Robert Burns	p35
22	B	Local councils are always elected.	p115
23	D	The Statute of Rhuddlan	p17
24	C	The United Nations	p125

PRACTICE TEST 20

1   Which of the following statements is correct?

   A   In 1979 Margaret Thatcher became the third woman to be Prime Minister of the UK.

   B   In 1979 Margaret Thatcher became the first woman to be Prime Minister of the UK.

2   The British fought a war in South Africa against settlers from the Netherlands. What were these settlers called?

   A   South Africans

   B   Boers

   C   Dutch

   D   Namibians

3   Who was William Wordsworth?

   A   A politician

   B   An engineer

   C   A sculptor

   D   A poet

4   Who was Henry VIII's first wife?

   A   Elizabeth of York

   B   Catherine Howard

   C   Catherine of Aragon

   D   Mary, Queen of Scots

5   Which of the following statements is correct?

   A   King Henry V led his army to victory at the Battle of Agincourt.

   B   Queen Victoria led her army to victory at the Battle of Agincourt.

6   What was the Duke of Wellington also known as?

   A   Field Marshal

   B   Iron Duke

   C   Bronze Duke

   D   Iron General

7   Which of the following statements is correct?

   A   Hugh Hudson is a film director who made *Chariots of Fire*.

   B   Hugh Hudson is an author who wrote *Brighton Rock* and *The Heart of the Matter*.

8   Which of the following is a UK city?

   A   Gothenburg

   B   Madrid

   C   Moscow

   D   Southampton

9   Which of these is a modern UK regional language?

   A   Celtic

   B   Latin

   C   Gaelic

   D   Kentish

10   Which of the statements below is correct?

   A   More women than men study at university.

   B   More men than women study at university.

11 What was Isambard Kingdom Brunel known for?

- **A** His work as an engineer
- **B** His work as a poet
- **C** His work as a nurse
- **D** His sporting achievements

12 Where is the Northern Irish Assembly?

- **A** Westminster
- **B** Stormont
- **C** Holyrood
- **D** The Senedd

13 Which part of London would you most associate with theatres?

- **A** The East End
- **B** The City
- **C** Canary Wharf
- **D** The West End

14 Where are the Crown Jewels kept?

- **A** Buckingham Palace
- **B** Tower of London
- **C** Hampton Court
- **D** Westminster Abbey

15 Which scientist, born in 1643, discovered that white light is made up of the colours of the rainbow?

- **A** Isaac Newton
- **B** Ernest Rutherford
- **C** Howard Florey
- **D** Sir Peter Mansfield

16   What do children do on Mothering Sunday?

  A Play 'trick or treat'

  B Give cards and gifts to their mothers

  C Go to school

  D Visit their grandparents

17   The BBC has organised which series of famous concerts since 1927?

  A The Proms

  B Aldeburgh Festival

  C The Edinburgh Festival

  D Summer season at Glyndebourne

18   What is the free press?

  A Newspapers distributed at no cost

  B Journalists who work without pay

  C Newspapers and other publications which are not under government control

  D Public access to printing services without cost

19   The judiciary is responsible for which TWO of the following?

  A Interpreting the law

  B Keeping order during political debates

  C Nominating peers

  D Making sure that trials are fair

20   During which period of British history was the railway engine pioneered, leading to a major expansion of the railways?

  A The Elizabethan period

  B The Georgian period

  C The Victorian period

  D The Jacobean period

21 What religion was Elizabeth I?

- **A** Catholic
- **B** Presbyterian
- **C** Protestant
- **D** Puritan

22 Who succeeded Oliver Cromwell following his death in 1658?

- **A** Charles I
- **B** Richard Cromwell
- **C** James II
- **D** Charles II

23 Which of these is a traditional pub activity?

- **A** Table tennis
- **B** Lectures
- **C** Jumble sales
- **D** Darts

24 What was the name of the first major railway constructed in Britain?

- **A** The Great Western Railway
- **B** The North-Eastern Railroad
- **C** The Southern Rail Link
- **D** The Eastern Expressway

ANSWERS: PRACTICE TEST 20

			Study material reference
1	B	In 1979 Margaret Thatcher became the first woman to be Prime Minister of the UK.	p58
2	B	Boers	p45
3	D	A poet	p87
4	C	Catherine of Aragon	p23
5	A	King Henry V led his army to victory at the Battle of Agincourt.	p17
6	B	Iron Duke	p39
7	A	Hugh Hudson is a film director who made *Chariots of Fire*.	p91
8	D	Southampton	p62–63
9	C	Gaelic	p64
10	A	More women than men study at university.	p66
11	A	His work as an engineer	p42
12	B	Stormont	p122
13	D	The West End	p81
14	B	Tower of London	p102
15	A	Isaac Newton	p31
16	B	Give cards and gifts to their mothers	p72
17	A	The Proms	p79
18	C	Newspapers and other publications which are not under government control	p33
19	A	Interpreting the law	p129
	D	Making sure that trials are fair	
20	C	The Victorian period	p41
21	C	Protestant	p25
22	B	Richard Cromwell	p30
23	D	Darts	p93
24	A	The Great Western Railway	p42

WELL DONE!

You've just taken 20 full tests.

Best of luck for your official Life in the UK test.

Let us know how it goes at
www.lifeintheuk.net/feedback

We'd love to hear your experiences, good or bad, or any suggestions you have to help us make our products better.

Get the BritTest app

Take practice tests wherever you go with
hundreds of questions and randomised
practice tests in your hand.

The essential revision aid for anyone on the move.
Find out more at **www.lifeintheuk.net/app.**